fig heaven

fig heaven

70 Recipes

for the World's Most

Luscious Fruit

marie simmons

WILLIAM MORROW

An Imprint of HarperCollinsPublishers

HarperCollins books may be purchased for educational, business, or sales promotional use. For information please write: Special Markets Department, HarperCollins Publishers Inc., 10 East 53rd Street, New York, NY 10022.

FIRST EDITION

Photographs by David Campbell

Illustration by Catherine Kirkwood

Printed on acid-free paper

Library of Congress Cataloging-in-Publication Data

Simmons, Marie.
    Fig heaven : 70 recipes for the world's most luscious fruit /
Marie Simmons.
        p.   cm.
    ISBN 0-06-053849-X
    1. Cookery (Figs)   2. Fig.   I. Title.
TX813.F5.S56   2004
641.6'437—dc22

                                                        2003057124

04 05 06 07 08 WBC/RRD 10 9 8 7 6 5 4 3 2

Thank you John,

    for moving me to fig heaven

contents

acknowledgments

My fig odyssey began when I discovered the fig man at our local farmers' market in El Cerrito, California. I bought too many figs that fateful Saturday morning and was forced to think beyond fresh fruit salad and prosciutto di Parma with figs. Looking at the pile of gorgeous figs sitting in a bowl on my kitchen counter, I started cooking—and embarked on a new food adventure. I wrote about the experience in my *Los Angeles Times* Syndicate column and then, with fig recipes to spare, I asked Richard Chapman, the culinary school coordinator at our local Sur la Table kitchenware store, if he thought a fig cooking class would be popular. When Richard said, "Let's try it," I was off and running.

To my surprise, Mike Emigh, president, and Linda Cain, vice-president of marketing, Valley Fig Growers in California, attended that first class. Afterward they invited me to spend a day in Madera County meeting fig growers and processors.

Right after my day in fig country I began to think about writing a fig cookbook. Many fig-lovers helped make my wish a reality.

Thank you, Richard, for saying yes to the class; and Linda and Mike for being so good at your jobs that you had to see what this fig class (and the teacher) was all about. Thank you Gary Jue, vice-president of marketing sales and technical services, Valley Fig Growers; Louise Ferguson, extension specialist, University of California, Kearney Agricultural Center; and Clay Weeks, horticulturist, and Dawn Kerbow, biological science technician, USDA National Clonal Germ Plasm Repository, for your help with my botanical queries. Thank you, Judith Weber, a warm, wise agent, who loved the idea from the beginning; Harriet Bell, one terrific editor, who didn't hesitate for a moment when I sheepishly admitted that I was thinking about writing a proposal for a fig cookbook; Lucy Baker, for her guidance; Carrie Bachman, for spreading the word; and Katherine Ness for excellent copyediting.

For contributing to my research, sharing recipes and fig lore, helping me to make contacts, or supplying me with figs—or for all of the above—I give heartfelt thanks to Jean Anderson, Michael Babcock, Juliann and Steve Beckendorf, Sondra Bernstein, Linda Carucci, Tony Di Dio, Jane Ellison, Bill Fore, Ed George, Yuk and Yonki Hamada, Paula Hamilton, Kevin Herman, Janie Hibler, Sharna Hoffman, Evan Kleiman, Kristi and Rick Knoll, Vianna La Place, Nadia Merzliakov, Rocky Palomino, Al Rehmke, Miriam Rubin, Debbie and Peter Rugh, Mary Etta Segerstrom, Michele Scicolone, Stacy Sussman, Dory and Tobias Tuma, and Heidi Yorkshire.

I am grateful to the California Fig Advisory Board and manager Ron Klamm for generously providing the photographs for my book, and to the photography team of Cherryl Bell, Stevie Bass, and David Campbell for the beautiful results. Thank you, Brooke Jackson, for expert help with recipe retests, and Aimee Male, for editorial assistance.

I thank my many friends and neighbors who never said, "No, thank you," when I asked them to be tasters for my many fig recipe attempts. Your responses always helped to make the painstaking process of recipe testing more fun than it should be.

introduction

I moved from Brooklyn, New York, to Richmond, California, five years ago. At first I missed my family and friends. I still miss them, but not as much as I used to. I think it's because of the figs.

I have never seen so many figs in one place in my life. Big mounds of them appear at our local farmers' market in June, and again in August through September—and, if the weather remains warm, into November. Plump greenish-yellow figs, small purplish-black ones, and shapely chartreuse figs, their rounded cheeks tinted with a blush of purple. Figs in more different sizes and shapes than I ever imagined, all mixed together. I am amazed that the farmers treat what I consider precious cargo with such nonchalance.

I stand back and watch early-morning market devotees gather tightly around the tables of figs. One hand after another gently selects a fig, cups it softly, and contemplates its worth. It either goes into the bag with the other selections or is gingerly returned to the pile. I watch, waiting eagerly for a space to clear so I can take part in this ritual.

On weekday mornings the market is not as busy as is it on Saturdays. I use this quiet time to quiz the farmers about varieties, taste, and ripeness. I am puzzled as to why some farmers don't sort the figs by variety and some do. One farmer explains that his orchard contains fig trees of different varieties, and putting them in one flat is easier for the pickers. One farmer, sensitive to my enthusiasm, takes the time to explain the different varieties to me and patiently answers my questions. But it is his demonstration of ripeness that leaves me weak in the knees. Carefully he picks up a fig and turns it over. "Here," he says, "is a perfectly ripe fig." There is a single teardrop of syrup oozing from its blossom end. (This, I later learned, is called the "eye" of the fig.) I am uncharacteristically speechless. Then he lifts another fig from the pile and offers it to me. It sits on my outstretched hand. It is warm from the sun and so heavy with sugar that its sides are literally bursting with rivulets of syrup.

Right then and there I have an epiphany: I'm in fig heaven.

• • •

My association of figs and heaven isn't all that far off the mark. "If I should wish a fruit brought to paradise, it would certainly be the fig," said the prophet Mohammed. In the book of Genesis, Adam and Eve stroll about the Garden of Eden, eat the forbidden fruit, and, self-conscious of their nakedness, "sewed fig leaves together, and made themselves aprons."

Much has been written about the historical significance of the fig. Figs are mentioned repeatedly in the Bible and throughout early history. Thought to be native to Asia Minor and western Asia, the fig migrated throughout the Middle East and the Mediterranean region, where it thrived. The early Egyptians, who ate figs both fresh and dried, buried baskets of figs alongside their dead to provide sustenance in the hereafter. Cleopatra, the Egyptian wife of Julius Caesar and Marc Antony's mistress, is said to have committed suicide by keeping a live asp hidden in a basket of figs and allowing it to bite her, presumably as she, with eyes turned toward the heavens, savored her favorite fruit.

To sink your teeth into a fig's soft, sweet, succulent center is one of the most sensually de-

"Prosciutto di Parma, eaten with . . . fresh figs, must be the most perfect hors d'oeuvre ever invented."
—A Book of Mediterranean Food, by Elizabeth David

lectable of experiences. The allure is in both its smooth texture and its sweet taste. The fig has the highest sugar content of all fruits and was used in ancient times as both a staple food and a sweetener. It was prized for its medicinal properties and was eaten as a training food by Greek athletes.

The early Romans fed their hogs figs to fatten them up and to sweeten their meat and livers. They fed geese figs, too, to fatten their livers for an early version of foie gras. In *De Re Coquinaria,* Apicius, the first-century Roman cook, includes a recipe for ham boiled with "25 dried figs." Today ham and figs remains a classic combination that has survived 2,000 years of cooks and gourmands.

Figs and Love

Legend has it that Bacchus, the infamous Roman and Greek god of wine and revelry (the Greeks called him Dionysus), celebrated the first fruits of the fig harvest with wild parties and orgies where the guests wore crowns of fig leaves and garlands of dried figs. For both the Greeks and the Romans, however, the fig was revered. The fruit was a metaphor for fertility, and it represented both male and female sexuality. The fig was, and still is, considered by some to be an aphrodisiac and is often associated with erotic and romantic love.

> *The fig is a very secretive fruit.*
> *As you see it standing growing, you feel at once it is symbolic:*
> *And it seems male.*
> *But when you come to know it better, you agree with the*
> *   Romans, it is female.*
>
> —From "Figs," by D. H. Lawrence

Fig Botany and Cultivation

The fruit-bearing fig tree, *Ficus carica,* belongs to the enormous mulberry family, Moraceae. It's the only member of the family that is cultivated for its fruit. Unique in the world of botany, the fig tree, unlike other fruit-bearing trees, does not burst into glorious blossoms before the fruit forms. Instead, the fig tree produces small hard green balls (called peduncles) that look like green olives; each peduncle grows into a pouch called the syconium. The interior of the syconium is lined with hundreds of tiny flowers, which will develop into drupelets. When we cut into a ripe fig, these minute flowers make up what we call the fig's pulp or soft center. Although considered a fruit, the fig is actually a flower that is inverted into itself.

Fig trees grow throughout the world in various shapes and sizes. There are hundreds of varieties, but not all are fruit-bearing. The banyan tree of eastern Asia, called the "world tree" because its tall branches are said to link earth to heaven, and the bodhi tree, known as the "tree of enlightenment" because it's where Buddha sat and studied, are both enormous fig trees. Other fig trees grow low to the ground like bushes or into twisted vinelike plants that wrap themselves around everything in sight. Trees in commercial orchards are pruned low so that the fruit is easy to harvest. While fig trees thrive best in warm climates, they do grow in some of the most unlikely locations.

A few generations back, some Italian immigrants brought fig tree cuttings with them to America. In cities such as Boston and Chicago, they lovingly planted their cuttings in a protected place in their gardens—perhaps against a wall with a southern exposure—to keep them warm. Or the cutting was planted in a large pot on casters, making it easy to move the tree inside during the freezing winters.

In Carroll Gardens, in Brooklyn, New York, my friend Tony has one of these "imported" trees. His grandfather brought their family's fig tree to Brooklyn from a small town in Sicily more than sixty years ago. Today the tree is more than twenty feet tall and bears such copious amounts of fruit that Tony gives it away all summer. Tony remembers his grandfather wrapping the tree in blankets in the winter. Once, when he was a kid, Tony asked him, "Why the blankets?" His grandfather said, "Because the tree thinks it's still in Sicily."

The Spanish first brought figs to Florida in the late 1500s, and records show that in 1787 Thomas Jefferson, then United States Minister to France, ordered cuttings sent to Monticello, in Virginia. Although fig trees were planted throughout the South and continue to grow in backyards today, a commercial crop was never developed there.

It was in the soil and climate of California that the fig began to truly thrive in North America. In 1769, the Franciscan missionary Father Junipero Serra planted fig trees at the Mission San Diego de Alcalá. Soon these dark black, intensely sweet figs, aptly named Black Mission figs, could be seen growing from San Diego north to Sonoma.

In the late 1880s industrious California farmers, looking for a tree that would produce a large, plump, dried fig to compete with imported figs, introduced the Sari Lop fig from Smyrna (now known as Izmir), Turkey. The dried fruit of this variety of fig was prized for its sweetness and its intensely nutty taste. But the first trees planted in California refused to produce edible fruit.

No one knew why until the process of *caprification* was revealed. A centuries-old method (ancient Greeks wrote about it in the 4th century B.C.), caprification is the process where branches of the wild fig, the caprifig, hanging with inedible fruit teaming with tiny wasps (practically invisible to the naked eye), are tied to cultivated trees that require pollination. Thousands of these tiny nonstinging female wasps, called *Blastophaga psenes*, set off in search of male figs where they can lay their eggs. They fly into the surrounding fig trees and in and out of figs (through the blossom end or "eye"), and transfer the male pollen collected on their wings to the female Sari Lop figs. Although the botanical structure of the female figs makes it impossible for the wasps to deposit their eggs there, all is not lost because the male pollen left behind pollinates the female figs. It's a bittersweet story because only about one in a few thousand tiny wasps ever succeeds in finding a male fig in which to deposit her eggs. Most of the wasps die within a day, but their plight leaves behind juicy ripe figs. Fig devotees owe a lot to these tiny wasps.

And so does California. The introduction of caprification was successful, and the Sari Lop fig trees helped to launch the California fig industry. The Sari Lop was renamed Calimyrna, for California, its new home, and Smyrna, its place of origin.

If you drive past a fig orchard, you can be certain the trees are Calimyrna if you see paper bags or baskets hanging in the trees. Inside these containers are male caprifigs swarming with tiny lady wasps about to begin their sad, but important, journey.

Not all figs need to be pollinated to ripen. Common (also called persistent) figs—including Black Mission, Brown Turkey, Kadota, and Adriatic—do not need pollination. There is also an intermediate group that occasionally needs pollination to set a main crop. This group includes King and San Pedro figs.

Today Turkey leads the world in fig production; California is third, only slightly behind Greece. In California there are approximately 14,000 acres of trees, primarily in the San Joaquin Valley, producing about 15,000 tons of figs. Most of these figs are dried. Only 20 percent of the harvest is sold fresh, although this percentage has doubled in the past five years. Because figs are so perishable, the majority of the world's crop is dried whole, with a large percentage ground into paste and sold for baked goods and confections.

Dried Figs

When I was growing up in the Hudson Valley, in New York State, the only figs I knew were dried. They were a special treat during the holidays when my mother added them, along with walnuts and almonds still in their shells, to the carefully arranged fruit bowl destined for the holiday dessert table. Even then I loved their moist, chewy centers and their crunchy texture. When the holidays were over, my grandmother used the leftover dried figs and nuts to make her famous stuffed cookies. A childhood favorite, they were kept in a canning pot in the sewing room, ready to be slipped into the pockets of her grandchildren when they stopped by for a visit (see page 119).

California figs are dried on the trees. The rows of trees, with their bare branches studded with wizened fruit reaching skyward in the blazing sun set against an azure sky, look like a Surrealist painting. The parched earth, the barren trees, and the fruit are tinted in various shades of ocher. As the figs drop to the ground they are harvested, sorted, washed, and then packaged.

The two most popular domestic dried figs are the small, intensely sweet Black Mission and the larger, nutty, and slightly crunchy Calimyrna. The Adriatic fig, prized for its sweet dried pulp, is ground to a paste and sold for cookie- and pastry-making. The Kadota fig, small and practically seedless, is preferred for canning and preserving.

Imported dried figs from Turkey, Greece, Spain, and Italy are similar to the Calimyrna. They are sometimes sold in rings threaded on raffia—a centuries-old tradition from the days when figs were a source of sustenance on long journeys.

Eaten plain, dried figs are a delectable treat. The abundance of sugar in the fig sometimes comes to the surface, leaving a coating of fine white crystals. Personally, I find the crunch of the sugar crystals satisfying, especially if I'm having a fig or two for a quick snack. But the sugar melts off when the figs are reconstituted. There are two methods for "plumping" dried figs. They can be lightly sprinkled with water and then warmed in the microwave for about 1 minute; or they can be simmered in wine, water, or fruit juice to cover, until absorbed, usually 10 to 20 minutes. As the figs cool, excess liquid is reabsorbed, making them even moister and juicier.

fig heaven

The easiest way to cut up a dried fig is with kitchen scissors. To avoid a sticky mess, lightly brush or spray the scissor blades with a little vegetable oil. The same vegetable oil application works when chopping figs in a food processor (make sure to cut the figs into ½-inch pieces first) or when chopping them with a knife. Another method is to freeze the figs for about an hour to firm them up, and then to rinse the knife frequently with hot water while slicing or chopping. Store opened packages of dried figs, tightly sealed so they won't get hard, either at cool room temperature or in the refrigerator.

Dried figs are a highly nutritious snack. They contain more fiber, both soluble and insoluble, than any other fruit, which is good for the digestion and promotes heart health by lowering cholesterol. One and a half ounces, or about 4 dried figs, contain about 120 calories. Figs provide vitamin B_6, vitamin E, potassium, calcium, iron, and antioxidant phytonutrients.

QUICK IDEAS FOR DRIED FIGS

WALNUT-STUFFED FIGS: Halve moist dried figs and push a generous piece of walnut into each soft center. Spread each fig with a smear of cream cheese.

CANDIED ORANGE-STUFFED FIGS: Cut a flap in the bottom of each fig and press on the soft inside to make a pocket. Insert a chunk of candied orange peel and replace the flap. Dip the figs in a combination of melted semisweet chocolate and unsalted butter (2 ounces, or squares, of chocolate to ½ ounce, or 1 tablespoon, of butter for about 12 figs).

CHEESE-STUFFED FIGS: Halve a moist dried fig and push a ½-inch chunk of Parmigiano-Reggiano, Grana Padano, Pecorino Romano, Asiago, Stilton, Dry Jack, Manchego, or other salty hard cheese into the center. Serve as they are, or wrap each fig in a ribbon of thinly sliced Black Forest ham, prosciutto di Parma, or other ham.

MARINATED FIGS: Plump 8 ounces dried figs in boiling salted water to cover for 10 minutes. Drain, and toss with a drizzle of olive oil, ½ teaspoon each of dried oregano, crushed fennel seeds, and grated orange zest, a pinch of kosher salt, and a grinding of black pepper. Marinate for 24 hours.

SOUSED FIGS: Plump dried figs in boiling red wine to cover for 15 minutes. Marinate in the wine overnight. Drain, and serve with cheese.

FIGS WITH GRAINS: Add diced moist dried figs to cooked white or brown rice, couscous, or pilaf.

FIGS WITH SALAD: Add sliced moist dried figs and toasted walnuts, hazelnuts, or almonds to a mixed green salad. Toss with a vinaigrette dressing.

FAST IDEAS FOR FRESH FIGS

FIGS AND PROSCIUTTO DI PARMA: Cut two small or one large fresh fig in half lengthwise and place it on a plate. Drape one large slice of thinly sliced proscuitto over the fig.

FIGS WITH GOAT CHEESE: Cut figs in half lengthwise. Press a piece of fresh basil into the soft center of each fig; add a ½-inch cube of fresh goat cheese. Drizzle with olive oil and add a grinding of black pepper.

FIGS ON THE GRILL: Cut figs in half lengthwise and grill, cut side down, for just 1 minute; then turn carefully with a wide spatula and grill 1 minute more. Tuck into a salad, add to a sandwich, or eat plain. Add a curl of cheese (Parmigiano-Reggiano, Asiago, French Comté). Or drizzle with a mixture of honey and lemon juice or olive oil and lemon juice. Add a few snips of rosemary, thyme, or basil, a few grains of kosher salt, and/or a few specks of freshly ground black pepper, if desired.

FIG CROSTINI: Mash a couple of ripe figs in a small bowl; drizzle with a teaspoon of honey; add a few grains of kosher salt. Spread on crostini (toasted Italian bread); consider these added toppings: a slice of prosciutto di Parma or Black Forest ham, cut to fit, or a sprinkling of crumbled ricotta salata.

SAUTÉED FRESH FIGS WITH BALSAMIC VINEGAR: Melt ½ tablespoon unsalted butter for each fig in a skillet until foamy; add halved figs, cut side down, and cook until golden. Turn cut side up and add a drop of aged balsamic vinegar to each fig. Serve warm as a side dish with roasted pork, lamb, duck, or squab or for dessert with a spoonful of mascarpone or softly whipped cream.

SIMPLE FIG DESSERT: Arrange halved ripe figs on a plate. Press a spoonful of mascarpone or Gorgonzola dolce into the center of each. Drizzle with honey.

BAKED FIGS: Cut figs in half lengthwise and place them cut side up, in a buttered baking dish. Sprinkle each fig with 1 teaspoon granulated sugar or light brown sugar. Bake in a 350°F oven for 30 minutes. Serve warm or chilled, with a puddle of heavy cream, a spoonful of fromage blanc, or a dollop of mascarpone alongside, for dessert.

FIGS WITH RASPBERRIES: Cut figs in half lengthwise. Press a spoonful of softened fresh goat cheese or mascarpone in the center of each half. Drizzle with a sweetened puree of fresh raspberries. Garnish each serving with whole fresh raspberries and a few blueberries. Serve for dessert.

fig heaven

Fresh Figs

My introduction to fresh figs occurred much later in life. As a college student I lived in Brooklyn, New York, where fresh figs would occasionally appear on restaurant menus or at upscale groceries. I don't remember where I tasted my first fresh fig, but I do remember the taste. I rejoiced at its sweetness and ethereal texture. It was love at first bite. And, like all first loves, it was never forgotten.

When fresh figs were in the market, I had to take one or two home with me, no matter what the cost, especially if they looked plump and juicy despite their journey across the country. (They were often priced by the piece, not the pound.) I served them simply: halved and draped with a paper-thin slice of prosciutto di Parma.

I think I was fig-deprived because I empathized with one of my favorite cookbook authors, British writer Elizabeth David, when I read in her book *Summer Cooking*: "Figs are so rare in this country that it is madness to do anything but eat them and be thankful." I did and I was.

Buying Fresh Figs

There is an Italian saying that goes like this, *"Il collo d'impiccato e la camicia da furfante,"* which means, "a ripe fig has a neck like a man who has been hanged, and an open shirt like a thief." In other words, when ripe the fig stem should be long, narrow, and slightly wrinkled, and the body of the fig should be literally bursting with syrupy sugar. This, of course, is the ideal. But when buying figs I am happy if the fig feels plump and heavy (and in the best of circumstances, warm) in my hand and gives ever so slightly to pressure from a fingertip. If there is a drop of syrup, or "tear in its eye," at the blossom end, it's ready to eat. Check each fig carefully to make sure it's free of mold. Very ripe figs should be consumed, if not immediately, one day after they are purchased. If figs are left sitting in the refrigerator for more than 2 or 3 days they'll begin to spoil. If the figs are under ripe when you buy them they will soften slightly if left at room temperature for 1 or 2 days. But in my experience if a fig is harvested when it's unripe it will never ripen properly.

The skin of a ripe fig is very delicate and should be handled gently. Store ripe figs in a single layer, without touching each other, on a paper-lined tray. If refrigerated, leave them uncovered or cover them loosely with a paper towel. My favorite way to store figs is in a loosely closed recycled egg carton.

Preparing Fresh Figs

Just before using the figs, gently rinse them in cool water, pat them dry with a paper or cloth towel, and trim off the stems. Figs only need to be peeled if the skin is thick and rough. There is an Italian saying: "Give the skin of the fig to your enemy and the skin of the peach to your friends." If using purple-skinned figs in a dish where the color might bleed—such as pasta, risotto, or a sauce—then the figs should be peeled. Use a small sharp knife to loosen the skin at the stem end and pull it down in a thin strip. The skin will come away from the flesh very easily. Do not peel the fig if you want it to retain its shape when cut. The skin helps to hold the soft flesh intact. Always cut fresh figs with a sharp knife with a long thin blade. Chopping will turn figs to mush. Cut fresh figs into dices, chunks, wedges, or halves.

Fresh Fig Varieties and Seasons

In warm climates some fig trees bear two crops: a small crop of large-sized fruit called the breba crop in June, followed by a more bountiful crop of medium-sized fruit from late July until mid-August. The latter crop will continue ripening as long as the weather is warm. In California figs are often available until Thanksgiving.

During fig season in California, the markets are filled predominately with Black Mission, Brown Turkey, Calimyrna, and Kadota figs. I can also find, in more limited quantity, the bright green Desert King, the sweet, juicy Adriatic, and the lovely green-striped Panaché.

A Fig Tasting

On a sweltering hot day one September, I traveled to Davis, California, to have lunch with friends and was introduced to Dory Tuma. Dory and her husband, Elias, a retired economics professor from University of California at Davis, have fifteen fig trees on their small acreage not far from Davis. It happened to be peak harvest time, and knowing about my fig book proposal, they generously packed up a selection of their figs for me to take home. What a bonanza! Talk about fig heaven! Here were fig varieties I had only read about in books, figs barely available commercially or at my farmers' market: tiny black ones, curvaceous yellow ones, and even striped ones, with names like Panache, Everbearing, St. Anthony, Celeste, Excel, Negronne, White Marseilles, and Magnolia. The next day, back home in the Bay Area, I invited friends to a fig tasting. We very seriously filled in the tasting sheets I had prepared describing the color, texture, and flavor of each of the figs.

I used these tasting notes to help prepare the following descriptions of fig varieties.

FIG VARIETIES

ADRIATIC: Large, with a curvaceous shape; yellow-green skin; rose-colored pulp; honey flavor; excellent fresh or dried as a paste for fig cookies and pastries.

ALMA: Small to medium pear shape; golden skin; amber pulp; mildly sweet; well adapted to the southeastern United States.

BLACK MISSION: Medium pear shape; purple-black skin; medium-pink pulp; intensely sweet; when dried, the fruit turns black; excellent fresh or dried.

BLANCHE: Medium turban shape; light green skin; white pulp; mildly sweet and delicate; hardy, well adapted to the southern United States. (Similar to Lattarula.)

BROWN TURKEY: Large elongated shape; purple-brown skin; pink to red pulp; mildly sweet; popular commercial variety; never dried; hardy tree does well in temperate climates.

CALIMYRNA: Large round, slightly flattened shape; yellow skin; amber pulp; rich, nutty flavor; excellent fresh or dried.

CELESTE: Small to medium size; light violet skin, red to amber pulp; jamlike texture and flavor; one of the hardiest trees for home gardens.

EVERBEARING: Medium size; purple skin; rose-colored pulp; sweet, rich flavor; very hardy; good in cool areas.

EXCEL: Medium size; round; yellow skin; amber pulp; mildly sweet; very hardy. (Kadota hybrid.)

KADOTA: Small to medium size; pale green skin; creamy amber pulp; rich flavor; excellent fresh or dried; minimum seeds; good for canning and preserving.

KING: Large size; bright green skin; deep strawberry pulp; mildly sweet.

LATTARULA: Medium to large size; yellow-green skin; white pulp; very sweet.

MAGNOLIA: Large turban shape; thick bronze-yellow skin; honey-colored pulp; rich figgy flavor.

NEGRONNE: Small to large size; black skin; deep red pulp; very sweet; hardy; well adapted to southern and southwestern United States; will grow in containers in cool areas. (Also called Bordeaux and Violette de Bordeaux.)

PANACHÉ: Small to medium size; unusual yellow with green stripes; deep strawberry-tinted pulp; very sweet; very old variety; most successfully grown in California.

SAINT ANTHONY: Medium to large size; yellow, vertically ridged skin; pale pink pulp; mildly sweet.

WHITE MARSEILLES: Medium to large size; yellow-green; honey-colored pulp; very sweet; called the "Italian honey fig." (Lattarula). Also called La Harula.

THE FIRST FIG

We stood in front of our kitchen sink and gazed admiringly at our fig tree. We planted it in the middle of our tiny backyard, and to our eyes it was splendid, all six feet and one dozen straggly branches. If pride and admiration could make a tree thrive, this one would someday be magnificent.

Soon the tips of the branches were covered with small green lumps. Dark green, slick leaves appeared overnight, as leaves are wont to do here in California, where once, much to my amazement, a dead stick used to shore up a sagging fuchsia transformed itself into a rosebush. Then one day we spotted a very large fig half hidden under a leaf. It was enormous, and it was the only one.

We made jokes about our one mutant fig. It looked rather obscene in comparison to the other little baby figs stuck to the limbs like so many big green olives. Its skin was already turning purple-bronze, the typical coloration of a Brown Turkey fig. But the fruit was hard as a rock. It would never ripen, or so we suspected.

We left home for a week's vacation, and when we returned late at night we immediately went to the backyard to check on the progress of our fig. There, by the light of a full moon, we could see that our firstborn fig was definitely rounder and softer. Sure enough, it felt like a baby's bottom when we took turns cupping it gently with an outstretched hand. We agreed: Tomorrow morning we would photograph our first fig. Then maybe, just maybe, we would pick it.

The next morning, as we sipped our cappuccino and gazed out our kitchen window, the tree came into focus. But wait. Where was our beloved fig, our fair-haired child, our super-sized jewel? Hiding under a leaf? Fallen to the ground?

We rushed outside to investigate. After a few very long minutes, my husband, John, pointed to the top of the fence behind the tree. There was our fig. One of its curvaceous chubby cheeks was perfect. The other was missing a chunk of flesh. Had a fig-filching squirrel thoughtlessly left the other half? Or had he left it to taunt us? Maybe he was politely not finishing everything on his plate? Or maybe our first fig was so very big and luscious that half of it had filled his little squirrel tummy and he had left the remaining half to share.

The Fig Leaf

My friend Debbie tells me that growing up in Longview, Texas, she and her little playmates picked the biggest fig leaves from their neighbors' trees and spent lazy summer afternoons

fig heaven

sewing them together to make costumes for dress-up play. Like Adam and Eve, these kids had a natural instinct for fashion.

If you've ever seen a fig tree, or a fig bush, you know that the leaves can be enormous. Grass-green, with a matte finish and rough texture like a cat's tongue, the fig leaf ranges from 4 to 10 inches wide, or even larger, certainly large enough to wear as "aprons" as was necessary in the Garden of Eden or to sew into costumes for summertime play. Different varieties sport leaves of slightly different size, color, and texture, but most of them are large enough to wrap around portions of fish, cheese, or poultry. Rick Knoll, of Knoll Farms in Brentwood, California, uses them to line his rice pot. My friend Michele shared anecdotal directions for a fig leaf syrup for ice cream. When heated, the fig leaf imparts a haunting, alluring taste to the food it comes in contact with. At first taste I detect nuts, then spice, or a hint of vanilla, or maybe sweet dried hay or freshly cut grass. The taste is elusive but clean and pleasant, and if you have access to fig leaves, worth investigating.

1. Wash the leaves in warm water with a little mild soap; rinse very well and pat them dry. Cut off the stems close to the leaf, and blot away any milky sap. The sap is resin-like and can be a skin irritant, so wash your hands carefully after harvesting and handling the leaves.

2. Blanching fig leaves renders them more pliant and easier to wrap around food. To blanch, fill a sauté pan or a wide, deep saucepan halfway with water and heat to a boil. Add about 4 leaves at a time and simmer for about 30 seconds. Remove with tongs and drain well.

3. Place the leaves, smooth side down, on a work surface, stem end nearest you. Cut the fish, cheese, or poultry to fit in the center of the leaf with room around the edges to fold and cover the food. Place the seasoned food in the center; working from the stem end, fold the leaf over the food; fold in on both sides, tucking the edges under the food; then roll the food tightly in the leaf. Secure the flap with a small metal skewer or toothpick, if desired, or simply place the roll flap side down when cooking. The outside of the leaf can be coated with olive oil if desired, but it's not necessary.

4. Fig leaf–wrapped food can be broiled, roasted, steamed, or grilled. The timing depends on the food, but usually 5 to 10 minutes at a high temperature is sufficient. Roast on an oiled baking sheet in a 400°F oven, or place under a preheated

broiler or on a hot grill; turn halfway through cooking. Test by pressing through the leaf. Fish or poultry will feel firm; cheese will feel soft.

5. To eat or not to eat the fig leaf is a good question. I find the cooked leaf too tough and chewy to be palatable. When it's used as a liner for food (see Salmon and Potatoes Roasted on Fig Leaves with Fresh Fig Salad, page 75), it becomes crisp and brittle.

6. If you like, cook fig leaf–wrapped fish or poultry a day before serving and refrigerate it overnight. Sitting in the leaf for this extended time, the food has a chance to absorb even more of its complex flavors. Unwrap it the next day and serve the food chilled or at room temperature, in a salad or as an appetizer.

> *"Michelangelo's nude giant has also been the victim of guardians of public morality who, in the middle of the 16th century, insisted on the addition of a metal loincloth made of 28 fig leaves—a prudishness repeated in 1995, when religious authorities in Jerusalem declined Florence's gift of a full-scale replica of 'David' unless its privates were similarly concealed."*
>
> —Ross King, the *New York Times*

appetizers

crostini with quick fig jam and warm herbed goat cheese

*M*ake this fresh fig jam ahead and keep it on hand for a quick and easy appetizer or snack. Use any fresh herb, or a mixture of herbs, to flavor the goat cheese. I like lemon thyme, rosemary, or lavender blossoms, if they're available, in any combination.

❧

1 pound ripe green figs, stems trimmed, diced

2 tablespoons sugar

1 baguette

Extra virgin olive oil

6 ounces fresh goat cheese, well chilled

Freshly ground black pepper

1 tablespoon fresh thyme leaves

1 teaspoon snipped fresh rosemary

1 teaspoon fresh lavender blossoms, or ½ teaspoon dried, if available

❧

1. Place the figs in a small saucepan or skillet. Add the sugar and 2 tablespoons water, and heat, stirring, to a boil. Cook, uncovered, over medium heat until the figs have softened and the mixture is very thick, about 10 minutes. Transfer the jam to a small bowl and set it aside until ready to serve. (The jam can be made 1 or 2 days ahead, covered, and refrigerated until ready to serve.)
2. Preheat the broiler or grill.

3. Cut the baguette into 12 long diagonal slices, each about 5 inches long and ½ inch thick. Lightly brush both sides of the slices with the olive oil. Arrange the bread on a baking sheet and broil, or place it on a cooking grate and grill, turning to brown the slices evenly, about 1 minute on each side. Set the crostini aside.

4. Preheat the oven to 350°F.

5. Cut the cold cheese into ¼-inch cubes and place them in a small ovenproof dish or in a pie plate. Drizzle with 2 tablespoons olive oil and black pepper to taste. Bake until the cheese is warm, 10 to 15 minutes. Sprinkle with the thyme, rosemary, and lavender, if available.

6. To serve, spread the fig jam on the toasts; top each with a spoonful of warm cheese. Arrange on a platter and serve.

dried fig and black olive spread for crostini

makes about 2 cups

The Jimtown Store, in Sonoma County, California, sells a unique fig and olive spread. One day, out of my supply of this favorite spread—and, I might add, long before this collection of recipes was even a twinkle in my eye—I made up my own version. It isn't the same as Jimtown's because in this version the figs are more dominant in flavor than the olives. I also added some grated orange zest and fresh garlic. I like it spread on crostini best, sometimes with a little crumbled feta or blue cheese. Smear some into celery boats or red pepper wedges for a quick afternoon snack.

❧

8 ounces dried Black Mission or Calimyrna figs, stems trimmed, quartered (about 1½ cups)

1 cup pitted Kalamata olives

1½ teaspoons fennel seeds, crushed with a mortar and pestle or the side of a heavy knife

1 teaspoon minced garlic

¼ teaspoon grated orange zest

⅛ teaspoon freshly ground black pepper

¼ cup extra virgin olive oil

crostini, for serving

2 to 4 ounces crumbled feta or blue cheese, optional

❧

1. Combine the figs and 1 cup water in a small saucepan. Heat to a boil. Cook, covered, over low heat until almost all of the liquid has been absorbed, about 20 minutes. Cool slightly.

2. Combine the figs, olives, fennel seeds, garlic, orange zest, and black pepper in a food processor. Process until pureed, stopping to scrape the sides of the container down once or twice. With the motor running, slowly add the olive oil. Transfer the mixture to a container or bowl, cover, and refrigerate until ready to serve.

3. To serve, place the spread in a small bowl with a butter knife, and surround it with crostini. Alternatively, spread it on the crostini and serve plain or with a little crumbled cheese on top.

cream cheese, dried fig, and walnut spread

makes about 1½ cups

*T*his simple cream cheese spread, made entirely in the food processor, reminds me of the cream cheese and date-nut-bread sandwiches I once relished at my favorite Chock Full o' Nuts coffee shop when I was in college. (They were so rich that they were sold by the half sandwich.) Spoon it into crisp endive leaves or celery boats, spread it on pear or apple slices, crackers, or toast, or make a half sandwich on whole-grain bread. Or, for a more sophisticated taste, try the smoked salmon variation. Hot-smoked salmon has a more pronounced salty, smoky taste than brined salmon, but either type will work.

❧

6 large dried Calimyrna figs, stems trimmed, quartered (see Note)

8 ounces cream cheese, at room temperature

¼ cup chopped walnuts

½ teaspoon kosher salt

2 tablespoons thinly sliced green scallion tops, optional

❧

1. Finely chop the figs in a food processor. Add the cream cheese and process until combined. Add the walnuts and salt; pulse just to blend. Scrape into a bowl. Add the scallions, if desired.
2. Serve the spread on crisped endive leaves (see page 36), celery boats, crackers, apple or pear slices, or toast, or use it as a sandwich spread.

cream cheese, dried fig, and walnut spread with smoked salmon: Add ¼ cup diced smoked salmon (about 2 ounces) to the food processor along with the walnuts and salt.

note: To finely chop figs in a food processor, lightly brush or spray the inside of the processor bowl and the metal blade with vegetable oil. If the figs are unusually dry, re-constitute them in boiling water for 10 minutes; drain and blot dry before chopping.

bacon-wrapped wine-poached dried figs

makes 4 to 6 servings

*S*erve these delightful little morsels with drinks before dinner. Put them together ahead of time and then just pop them into the oven right before serving. Or keep the wine-poached figs on hand in the refrigerator, then stuff them, wrap them in bacon, and roast just a few or the full recipe, as needed.

12 large dried Black Mission or Calimyrna figs (about 8 ounces), stems trimmed

1½ cups red wine

1 sprig fresh rosemary, or 1 bay leaf

6 slices thick-cut bacon, halved crosswise

4 ounces Stilton, Roquefort, Cheddar, or Parmigiano-Reggiano cheese,
cut into ½-inch chunks

1. Combine the figs, wine, and rosemary in a medium saucepan and heat to a boil. Cook, covered, over low heat until the figs have softened, 20 to 25 minutes. Then uncover and boil gently until almost all the wine has evaporated. Allow to cool in the saucepan.

2. Fill a small saucepan halfway with water and heat to a boil. Add the bacon and boil for 5 minutes. Drain.

3. Preheat the oven to 400°F.

4. As you remove the figs from the saucepan, reserve any remaining reduced wine. Make a slit in the side of each fig, and push a cube of cheese into the soft center. Wrap a piece of ba-

con around each stuffed fig and fasten it with a toothpick or a small metal skewer. Place the figs in a small baking dish.

5. Bake until the bacon is browned, turning the figs over halfway through the baking time, 15 to 20 minutes total. Remove the baking dish from the oven and drizzle any reserved reduced wine over the figs.

6. Allow to cool slightly. Serve warm or at room temperature.

dried fig and cheese cocktail crescents

*S*erve these flaky sweet-and-salty little crescents with drinks before dinner. The cream cheese and butter pastry is fabulously rich but very easy
to make. (It's an excellent all-purpose enclosure for all sorts of tasty little
nibbles.) Top the fig mixture with your choice of cheese. Fresh goat cheese
makes a creamy filling; crumbled Stilton produces a salty, tangy filling.

❧

4 ounces cream cheese, cut into small pieces

8 tablespoons (1 stick) unsalted butter, cut into small pieces, at room temperature

1 cup all-purpose flour

½ teaspoon salt

4 ounces dried Calimyrna or Black Mission figs, stems trimmed, coarsely chopped
(about ½ cup packed)

½ cup coarsely chopped walnuts

4 ounces goat cheese or Stilton, well chilled, crumbled (about 1 cup)

1 egg yolk beaten with 1 tablespoon milk or heavy cream

❧

1. Combine the cream cheese, butter, flour, and salt in the bowl of a food processor. Pulse just until a dough forms; if needed, add ice water, 1 tablespoon at a time, to hold the dough together. Turn the dough out on a sheet of aluminum foil. With floured hands, gather it into a ball and flatten it into a disc. Wrap, and refrigerate until well chilled, 1 to 2 hours.
2. Combine the figs and ¼ cup water in a small saucepan and heat to a boil. Reduce the heat to very low, cover, and cook until the water has been absorbed, about 5 minutes. Allow to

cool. Puree the figs in a food processor. Transfer the puree to a bowl, stir in the walnuts, and set it aside.

3. Preheat the oven to 350°F.

4. Divide the chilled dough in half. Roll one half out on a lightly floured pastry cloth, using a rolling pin covered with a floured stocking, until you have a ⅛-inch-thick round. Using a biscuit cutter or a glass dipped in flour, cut out 3-inch rounds. Place 2 rounded teaspoons of the fig mixture just below the center of each one, and top with approximately 1 teaspoon cheese.

5. Wet the edges of each pastry round with a pastry brush or a fingertip dipped in water. Fold the round in half, and press the edges together with floured fingertips to make crescents. Stack and re-roll any scraps of dough.

6. Repeat with the remaining half of the dough, filling, and cheese.

7. Arrange the crescents on lightly buttered baking sheets, and brush the tops lightly with the egg yolk and milk mixture.

8. Bake until golden, about 15 minutes. Cool on a wire rack. Serve warm or at room temperature. These are best eaten within 4 to 5 days. (They freeze well: Reheat, still frozen, on a baking sheet in a preheated 350°F oven for 15 minutes.)

FIGS AND CHEESE: MORE FIG HEAVEN

The soft texture, sweet flavor, and slightly herbaceous quality of the fig pairs perfectly with many types of cheese, especially those with a slightly salty and tangy taste. Here are my favorite cheeses to combine with either fresh or dried figs.

Fresh or aged chèvre (goat cheese)

Ricotta, crème fraîche, fromage blanc, mascarpone

Feta, ricotta salata, young Pecorino Toscano

Parmigiano-Reggiano, Grana Padano, Pecorino Romano, Dry Jack, aged Gouda, Manchego, Capricious, English or domestic Cheddar

Gruyère, Comté, Fontina, Morbier, Humbolt Fog

Stilton, domestic blue, Roquefort, aged Gorgonzola, Gorgonzola dolce

cheese-filled fresh figs

These make a quick and easy, but elegant, hors d'oeuvre. Serve the figs simply stuffed with a small chunk of cheese, or for a more elaborate presentation, wrap each fig in a narrow ribbon of prosciutto di Parma. Rather than be deprived of such a delicacy when figs are out of season, see the variation below for a dried fig version. If you are lucky enough to have a fresh fig tree in your yard (or in your neighborhood), use the leaves to line the serving tray (see Note).

❧

8 large firm ripe figs, any variety, stems trimmed, halved lengthwise

Extra virgin olive oil

Snipped fresh rosemary

Kosher salt and freshly ground black pepper

4 ounces (approximately) Parmigiano-Reggiano, Grana Padano, Stilton, aged Gouda, Camembert, ricotta salata, chilled fresh goat cheese, or another of your favorite cheeses, or a combination, cut into sixteen ½-inch chunks

4 to 6 thin slices prosciutto di Parma, cut into 1-inch ribbons, optional

❧

1. Place the figs, cut side up, on a serving tray. Drizzle each fig with about ¼ teaspoon olive oil, a few snipped rosemary leaves, a few grains of salt, and a few bits of black pepper.
2. Gently push a chunk of cheese into the center of each fig. Wrap each fig in a ribbon of prosciutto, if using. Serve at room temperature.

note: Before using the fig leaves, wash them in warm water and mild soap and then rinse with cold water; pat dry with a towel.

dried fig version: Use 8 large, plump dried figs. (If the figs are too dry, plump them in boiling water for 10 minutes; then drain.) Leaving the figs whole, trim the stems. Make a slit in the side of each fig and push a piece of the cheese into the slit. Place the stuffed figs in a bowl and drizzle with 2 teaspoons extra virgin olive oil, the rosemary, salt, and pepper. Toss. Wrap each fig in a ribbon of prosciutto, if desired. Serve while warm or at room temperature.

grilled fresh figs on rosemary skewers

makes 4 servings

There are endless ways to serve these skewered honey-glazed figs. Try them hot off the grill as an appetizer, accompanied by small chunks of sharp aged Gouda, Cheddar, aged goat cheese, or Dry Jack, a favorite cheese from California. Sometimes I serve the warm figs, still on their skewers, on a bed of lightly dressed salad greens sprinkled with grated Parmigiano-Reggiano, or draped with a thin slice of prosciutto di Parma or Black Forest ham. They also make a nice snack accompanied by thinly sliced ham or salami, slivered crisped fennel (see page 47, Step 2) and black olives. I use them to garnish fig risotto, grilled meats, pan-seared duck breasts, Cornish hens, or roasted chicken. To keep the rosemary sprigs from burning, soak them in cold water before skewering the figs.

❧

4 stems fresh rosemary, each about 6 inches long

4 large firm ripe figs, any variety, stems trimmed, halved lengthwise

¼ cup honey

1 tablespoon fresh lemon juice

Freshly ground black pepper

❧

1. Strip the leaves from the bottom of the rosemary stems, leaving about 1 inch of leaves at the tip. Finely chop 2 teaspoons of the stripped rosemary leaves and set them aside.
2. Place the stems in a bowl and add cold water to cover; soak for at least 30 minutes. Drain the stems and blot them dry.

3. Skewer 2 fig halves crosswise on each rosemary stem. Arrange the skewers, with the cut sides of the figs facing up, on a plate. Stir the honey and lemon juice together in a small bowl, and brush the honey mixture over the cut sides of the figs.

4. Preheat the broiler or grill.

5. Grill or broil the figs until they are lightly browned and softened, 1 to 2 minutes per side. Sprinkle evenly with the reserved rosemary leaves and some black pepper.

6. Serve, on the skewers, while still warm.

roasted figs with gorgonzola and prosciutto di parma

makes 8 servings

*T*his outrageously delicious recipe has been making the rounds of innumerable restaurant menus for several years now. I haven't a clue which chef deserves credit for devising such a brilliant appetizer, but it's a memorable dish. If you're not a Gorgonzola fan, experiment with other cheeses, such as fresh goat cheese, Stilton, or Humbolt Fog, a firm goat's-milk cheese with a creamy finish, made in Northern California.

❦

8 large firm ripe figs, any variety, stems trimmed
8 cubes (about ½ inch) Gorgonzola cheese
8 thin slices prosciutto di Parma
8 radicchio leaves

❦

1. Preheat the oven to 500°F.
2. Cut an X in the top of each fig, slicing about ½ inch deep. Pull the four corners open and insert a cube of cheese into each fig. Wrap a slice of prosciutto around each of the figs, overlapping the edges. Place the figs in a large baking dish.
3. Roast until the prosciutto is crisp on the edges and the figs are warmed through, 10 to 12 minutes. Place a radicchio leaf on each salad plate, and place a fig in the center of each leaf. Serve hot.

fresh fig and asiago cheese frittata

makes 6 to 8 servings

*S*weet fresh figs, slightly tangy young Asiago cheese, and some mildly salty prosciutto provide the perfect balance in this unusual frittata. If a young or soft-textured mild Asiago is not available, use Fontina, Havarti, Monterey Jack, Teleme, or another semi-soft, mild cheese with a slight tang. Because the filling is chunky, I find it easier to finish cooking the frittata under the broiler rather than turning it over in the pan. Cut the frittata into thin wedges and serve it at room temperature with a chilled crisp white wine before dinner. Alternatively, cut the frittata into large wedges and serve it hot, with a salad of bitter greens tossed with a thin drizzle of balsamic vinegar, for lunch.

❦

2 tablespoons extra virgin olive oil

½ cup slivered onion

10 large eggs

1 teaspoon kosher salt

Freshly ground black pepper

4 slices prosciutto di Parma, snipped into ½-inch pieces with kitchen shears

10 firm ripe figs (a mixture of sizes and colors, if available), stems trimmed, halved if small and quartered if large

About 2 ounces young Asiago cheese (see headnote), cut into ¼-inch dice (½ cup)

❦

1. Heat the oil in a large (10-inch) ovenproof skillet, preferably nonstick, over medium heat. Add the onion and cook, stirring, until golden brown, about 5 minutes.
2. Meanwhile, whisk the eggs, $\frac{1}{4}$ cup water, salt, and a generous grinding of black pepper together in a large bowl until blended. Add this to the hot skillet and cook over medium-low heat until the eggs just begin to set on the bottom and around the edges, about 5 minutes. Lift the sides of the frittata and tilt the pan so that the raw center flows to the edges. Repeat at least two more times at different places around the edge of the frittata.
3. Sprinkle the prosciutto over the frittata (the center will still be undercooked) and then place the fig pieces evenly over the surface. Cook, covered, over low heat until the frittata is set, about 10 minutes.
4. Meanwhile, preheat the broiler.
5. Uncover the frittata and sprinkle it evenly with the cheese. Broil just until the top is golden, about 2 minutes.
6. Let the frittata stand for a few minutes before serving. To serve, loosen the edges and slide the frittata onto a large platter. Cut it into wedges and serve warm or at room temperature.

red pepper and dried fig sauce over ricotta salata

*R*icotta salata is salted ricotta cheese that has been aged and pressed until it is firm enough to slice with a knife. The heat and spice of dried red pepper, the sweetness of the fig sauce, and the saltiness of the ricotta salata all come together beautifully in this first course. The cold grapes and the slice of fresh orange tame the heat of the sauce. The sauce can be made ahead, but it's best served warm or at room temperature.

❧

8 ounces dried Calimyrna or Black Mission figs, stems trimmed, cut up
(about 1¼ cups packed)

One 3-inch cinnamon stick

¼ to ½ teaspoon dried red pepper flakes

2 tablespoons balsamic vinegar

½ teaspoon kosher salt

One 8-ounce wedge ricotta salata

2 strips orange zest, about ½ × 2 inches, cut into long thin threads

4 clusters seedless green grapes, well chilled

Two ½-inch-thick orange slices, halved

❧

1. Combine the figs, 2 cups of water, the cinnamon stick, and the red pepper flakes in a medium saucepan and heat to a boil. Cook, covered, over low heat until the figs are softened and all but 2 tablespoons of the liquid has been absorbed, 25 to 30 minutes. (If too

much liquid remains, simmer uncovered to evaporate the excess.) Allow to cool. Remove the cinnamon stick.

2. Combine the figs and their liquid, the vinegar, and the salt in the bowl of a food processor and process until chunky smooth. The sauce should be thick but not stiff. If it's too stiff, stir in 1 tablespoon warm water.

3. To serve, place the cheese on its side and cut slices from either end to make 12 triangles, each about ¼ inch thick. Place 3 triangles on each salad plate. Spoon about 1 tablespoon of the fig sauce onto the center of each triangle. Top with a few threads of orange zest. Garnish each plate with a cluster of grapes and a half-slice of orange, and serve at room temperature.

endive leaves with fresh fig salsa and goat cheese

makes 6 to 8 servings

*F*or this salad select the firmest green-skinned figs you can find. (The skins of purple figs turn the cheese pink.) Fold the ingredients very gently so the figs and cheese are not mashed together.

❧

2 heads Belgian endive

1 cup trimmed and diced firm ripe green figs

1 tablespoon minced red onion

1 tablespoon fresh lime juice

1 tablespoon minced fresh basil, plus more for garnish

½ teaspoon grated lime zest

Kosher salt and freshly ground black pepper

½ cup crumbled well-chilled goat cheese (about 4 ounces)

❧

1. Trim the stems and remove the cores from the endive; separate the leaves, trimming the stem as needed to separate the leaves without breaking them. You should have 16 or more large whole leaves. Place the leaves in a large bowl; add a cupful of ice and cold water to cover. Let stand while preparing the salsa.

2. Combine the figs, red onion, lime juice, 1 tablespoon basil, lime zest, a pinch of salt, and a grinding of black pepper. Fold to blend. Add the goat cheese and toss gently to blend.

3. Drain the crisped endive leaves, and blot them dry on a clean kitchen towel. Arrange them on a platter and fill each one with a spoonful of salsa. Garnish each with a piece of torn basil leaf, and serve immediately.

sandwiches, breads, and salads

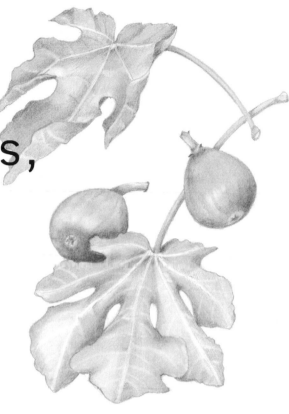

fresh fig quesadillas

makes 4 servings

*Q*uesadillas lend themselves to all sorts of interesting interpretations. A friend enjoyed fig quesadillas at a cocktail party and insisted that I experiment with the idea. The sweet warm figs and tangy melted cheese are a perfect filling in this popular Mexican dish. Use a tangy Spanish Manchego, aged Cheddar, California Dry Jack, Monterey Jack, or other cheese with good melting properties.

❧

1½ tablespoons extra virgin olive oil

Four 9-inch flour tortillas

2 cups (about 8 ounces) coarsely shredded cheese

1 cup trimmed and diced firm ripe green or black figs (about 8 ounces, or 6 large figs)

2 tablespoons minced red onion

2 tablespoons minced fresh cilantro

❧

1. Preheat the oven to 350°F. Brush a large baking sheet with the olive oil.

2. Place the tortillas on the baking sheet. Spread ¼ cup of the cheese on the bottom half of each tortilla. Add a layer of figs, using ¼ cup for each tortilla. Sprinkle each with about ½ tablespoon of the red onion and ½ tablespoon of the cilantro, and top with ¼ cup of the remaining cheese. Fold the tortillas over to make half-circles; press down lightly.

3. Bake until the tortillas are golden brown on the bottom, about 8 minutes. Using a wide spatula, turn the tortillas over; bake until the bottoms are golden brown, about 3 minutes. Remove the baking sheet from the oven and allow to cool slightly. Then transfer the quesadillas to a cutting board and use a knife or scissors to cut each one into 4 wedges. Serve warm.

open-faced dried fig and melted cheese sandwiches

*I*nspired by my love of cheese and figs, I concocted this open-faced sandwich using a simple dried fig "jam" and slivers of my favorite cheese of the moment. I originally used French Comté, a smooth, nutty, full-flavored type of Gruyère, but if it's not available, a well-aged Gruyère, Fontina, Stilton, or even a mild Cheddar is a good substitute. If you are feeling carnivorous, fry up some halved strips of bacon and lay them over the fig mixture before adding the cheese. This recipe makes four sandwiches but is easily scaled down to make just one. It makes a nourishing winter lunch with some salad greens on the side. The jam will keep, covered, in the refrigerator for a couple of weeks—ready and waiting for your next fig-and-melted-cheese-sandwich attack!

❧

8 ounces dried Calimyrna or Black Mission figs, stems trimmed, quartered (about 1½ cups)

Four ¼- to ½-inch-thick slices whole-grain rustic bread

4 to 6 ounces Comté, Gruyère, Fontina, or mild Cheddar cheese

❧

1. Combine the figs and 1 cup of water in a small saucepan and heat to a boil. Cook, covered, over low heat until almost all of the water has been absorbed and the figs are softened, 20 to 25 minutes. Cool slightly.
2. Transfer the figs to the bowl of a food processor and process until chunky smooth. Transfer the "jam" to a plastic container with a tight-fitting lid, and refrigerate until ready to use.
3. Preheat the broiler.

4. Lightly toast the bread on both sides either in the broiler or in a toaster. Spread one side of the bread with a thick layer (2 tablespoons or more, depending on the size of the slice) of the fig jam.
5. Use a sharp knife or a cheese plane to cut off thick slivers of cheese, and lay them on top of the jam. Place the sandwiches on a pan and heat under the broiler until the cheese is soft and bubbly, 1 to 2 minutes.
6. Cut into pieces and serve at once.

FIG SANDWICHES

GRILLED PIG N' FIG: Add a layer of sliced fresh figs to a grilled ham and cheese sandwich. Choose thinly sliced Teleme, Camembert, Gruyère, Fontina, or Monterey Jack for the cheese, and layer with a slice of baked or cured ham.

OPEN-FACED FIGS AND CHEESE: Spread a thin diagonal slice of baguette with a creamy cheese (cream cheese, fresh goat cheese, Teleme, Camembert, Brie, Saint André, or Gorgonzola); add a layer of thickly sliced fresh figs and a few pieces of torn basil.

FIG AND PROSCIUTTO PANINI: Layer one half of a soft sandwich roll with thick slices of fig. Toss some arugula with a drizzle of olive oil, a squirt of lemon juice, and a few grains of kosher salt. Place the arugula on top of the figs. Top with a folded slice of prosciutto and the other half of the roll.

fresh or dried fig, walnut, and rosemary focaccia

makes 6 to 8 servings

*P*eople often ask me to explain the difference between focaccia dough and pizza dough. Focaccia dough is made with more olive oil and water, resulting in a wetter dough. It also requires a double rising, which gives the bread more air holes and a chewier texture than pizza has. The olive oil taste is distinctive in focaccia, so use a full-flavored, fruity oil. In this version, topped with either fresh or dried figs, a small amount of sugar is added to the dough to complement the sweetness of the figs.

❧

⅓ cup fruity extra virgin olive oil

2 tablespoons coarsely chopped fresh rosemary

1½ cups warm water (105° to 115°F)

1 package active dry yeast

3¾ cups unbleached all-purpose flour

2 tablespoons sugar

3 teaspoons kosher salt

4 to 6 large green or purple figs, trimmed, or 8 to 10 moist dried figs (see Note), stems trimmed

¾ cup broken walnuts

❧

1. Combine the olive oil and 1 tablespoon of the rosemary in a small saucepan. Warm over low heat, about 1 minute. Remove from the heat and allow to cool.

2. Place the warm water in a large bowl; sprinkle with the yeast. Cover with plastic wrap and let stand until the yeast is creamy and dissolved, about 5 minutes.

3. Stir the cooled oil and rosemary, the flour, the sugar, and 2 teaspoons of the salt into the yeast mixture. Stir until a soft dough forms.

4. Turn the dough onto a lightly floured surface and knead until it is smooth and elastic, about 10 minutes. The dough should be sticky, do not add extra flour. To prevent excessive sticking, flour your hands and use a scraper or a flat spatula to free the dough from the work surface.

5. Oil the inside of a large bowl. Shape the dough into a ball and place it in the bowl; turn to coat with the oil. Cover the bowl with plastic wrap and let the dough rise in a warm place until doubled in bulk, about 1½ hours.

6. Punch the dough down. Transfer it to a generously oiled 15½ × 10½ × ¾-inch sheet pan. Flatten the dough with your hands and gently stretch, lift, and pat it evenly into the pan; press out any air bubbles. Cover it with plastic wrap and let it rise in a warm place until doubled in bulk, about 1 hour.

7. Position the oven rack in the lower third of the oven (not directly on the bottom), and preheat the oven to 400°F.

8. Cut the figs into twenty-four ¼-inch-thick rounds.

9. Use your fingertips to make 24 evenly spaced (4 across and 6 down) deep indentations in the dough. Press a fig slice into each of the indentations. Sprinkle the walnuts over the surface and press them lightly into the dough. Sprinkle with the remaining 1 tablespoon rosemary leaves and 1 teaspoon salt.

10. Bake until the top is golden and the edges are browned, 20 to 25 minutes. Let stand for 10 minutes. Then loosen the edges of the focaccia from the pan and slide it onto a wire rack. Serve warm or at room temperature, cut into squares.

note: If the figs are very dry, reconstitute the whole figs in boiling water for 10 minutes; then drain, blot dry, and slice.

grilled fresh fig, olive, and caramelized onion flatbreads

makes 6 servings

*F*latbreads are basically focaccia or pizza dough that has been shaped into an oval. For grilling, I shape the dough into 6 ovals. But, for baking (see Variation), the dough can be shaped into one whole flatbread or individual ones. For best results use a pizza stone or quarry tiles in your oven. Make your own pizza dough following the recipe, or take the easy way out and buy prepared dough, now available fresh in many markets.

❧

¼ cup extra virgin olive oil, plus more for brushing the flatbreads

6 cups thinly sliced onions (lengthwise slices)

Kosher salt and freshly ground black pepper

1 tablespoon minced fresh oregano

Pizza Dough (recipe follows), prepared through Step 3, or 2 pounds store-bought fresh or frozen pizza dough, proofed according to the package directions

Yellow cornmeal, for the cookie sheets

½ cup coarsely chopped pitted Kalamata olives

8 ounces Manchego, Asiago, fresh mozzarella, smoked mozzarella, or feta cheese, or a combination, cut into thin slices or slivers

8 to 10 firm ripe figs, any variety, stems trimmed, cut into ¼-inch-thick rounds

❧

1. Heat the ¼ cup oil in a large skillet, add the onions and cook, stirring, over medium-high heat until they are sizzling. Reduce the heat to medium-low and cook, stirring occasionally,

until the onions are golden and browned on the edges, about 20 minutes. Add salt, pepper, and the oregano. Remove from the heat and set aside.

2. Punch the dough down and divide it into 6 evenly sized portions. On a lightly floured surface, flatten and stretch each portion of dough into an oval 6 to 8 inches long and about 5 inches wide. Sprinkle two or three cookie sheets with yellow cornmeal, and place the dough on the cookie sheets. Cover the dough with clean kitchen towels and let it rise until soft and puffy, about 30 minutes.

3. Preheat the grill.

4. Brush the dough lightly with olive oil. Grill over indirect heat, oiled side down, uncovered, until the bottoms are golden brown, 3 to 5 minutes. Turn them over and grill on the other side until lightly brown, about 2 minutes. Transfer the flatbreads to the cookie sheets.

5. Quickly distribute the caramelized onions evenly over the flatbreads. Add a few olives to each, cover with overlapping slices of cheese, and then top with the fig slices. Grill covered until the cheese has melted and the bottoms of the flatbreads are browned and crisp, 6 to 8 minutes. Serve at once.

oven-baked fresh fig, olive, and caramelized onion flatbread

1. Prepare the Pizza Dough (recipe follows).

2. Place a pizza stone or quarry tiles on a rack in the lower third of the oven and preheat the oven to 500°F.

3. Punch the dough down and shape into a ball; let it rest for 10 minutes. Roll the dough into a 12-inch oval about ½ inch thick. Slide onto a pizza peel or a baking sheet sprinkled lightly with cornmeal.

4. Top evenly with the caramelized onions, the olives, the cheese slices, slightly overlapping, and the fig slices.

5. Transfer the flatbread from the pizza peel to the pizza stone or place the baking sheet on the pizza stone and bake until golden brown, about 15 minutes. Cut into 2-inch-wide strips and serve.

pizza dough

❧

1¼ cups warm water (105° to 115°F)

1 package active dry yeast

1 teaspoon sugar

2 tablespoons extra virgin olive oil

2 teaspoons salt

3½ to 4 cups unbleached all-purpose flour, or more as needed

❧

1. Combine ¼ cup of the warm water with the yeast and the sugar in a large bowl; stir to blend. Cover with plastic wrap and let stand until foamy, about 10 minutes.

2. Mix in the remaining 1 cup warm water, the olive oil, the salt, and 1½ cups of the flour, and stir until smooth. Gradually add the remaining 2 to 2½ cups flour, stirring, until the dough comes away from the sides of the bowl.

3. Turn the dough out onto a floured surface and knead until it is smooth and elastic, about 10 minutes, adding as much extra flour as needed to keep the dough from being too sticky. Shape the dough into a ball and place it in a large oiled bowl. Turn the dough to coat with the oil. Cover the bowl with plastic wrap and let the dough rise in a warm place until doubled in bulk, about 1 hour.

4. Punch the dough down and divide and shape as directed in the recipe. If not using the dough right away, punch it down, put it back in the bowl, cover lightly with plastic wrap, and refrigerate for up to 24 hours.

fig heaven

dried fig, orange, fennel, and sweet onion salad with mixed greens

makes 4 servings

This refreshing salad is perfect for perking up winter menus. If you like, you can poach the figs in the orange juice a day or two before serving.

❧

8 ounces dried Black Mission or Calimyrna figs (12 to 14 figs), stems trimmed

1 cup orange juice

¼ teaspoon fennel seeds, crushed with a mortar and pestle or the side of a heavy knife

1 fennel bulb (about 12 ounces)

2 large seedless oranges

2 tablespoons extra virgin olive oil

2 tablespoons sherry vinegar

½ teaspoon minced garlic

⅛ teaspoon kosher salt

Freshly ground black pepper

2 tablespoons minced red onion

6 cups mixed baby greens

2 paper-thin slices red onion, separated into rings

❧

1. Combine the figs, orange juice, and fennel seeds in a small saucepan and heat to a boil. Cook, covered, over low heat until the figs are soft and the juice is reduced to 2 table-

spoons, 20 to 25 minutes. Transfer to a bowl and refrigerate until chilled. This step can be done 1 or 2 days before serving.

2. Cut the fennel in half lengthwise; place the halves cut side down, and slice into thin half-circles. Finely chop 2 tablespoons of the fernlike fronds and reserve them. Place the fennel slices in a bowl of iced water and let stand for at least 20 minutes. Then drain and blot dry.

3. Grate ½ teaspoon zest from one of the oranges, and set it aside. Cut the peel and the white pith from the oranges. Working over a bowl to catch the juice, cut between the membranes with a small sharp knife to release the segments.

4. In a large bowl, combine 2 tablespoons of the fresh orange juice (reserve the remainder for another use) and the 2 tablespoons reserved fig juices with the olive oil, vinegar, garlic, salt, a grinding of pepper, and the reserved grated zest; whisk to blend.

5. Gently toss the orange segments, minced onion, and reserved fennel fronds together in a medium bowl. Drizzle with 1 tablespoon of the dressing and set aside.

6. Add the salad greens and the fennel slices to the dressing and toss to coat.

7. Divide the salad among 4 salad plates. Spoon the orange and onion mixture over the salad greens. Halve the figs and distribute them evenly among the plates. Garnish with the onion rings, and serve.

warm fresh fig salad with comté cheese and black forest ham

*P*retty, graceful, *and* luscious *are all adjectives I've heard others use to describe this salad, but I'm equally impressed with its simplicity, especially in the heat of summer. If the grill isn't on for other courses, the figs can be served at room temperature, but for this version we'll assume the grill is fired up. Slightly heating the figs brings out their natural sweetness. For the salad, use a mixture of baby salad greens with a few nasturtiums or other edible flowers tossed into the mix. Make sure the ham is the best quality available and sliced paper-thin.*

4 large firm ripe figs, any variety, stems trimmed, halved lengthwise

3 tablespoons extra virgin olive oil, plus extra for brushing the figs

2 teaspoons minced fresh rosemary

8 large curls of Comte or aged Gruyère cheese, cut with a cheese plane or a sturdy vegetable peeler

1 tablespoon herb-flavored wine vinegar or fresh lemon juice

Freshly ground black pepper

Pinch of kosher salt

6 cups lightly packed mixed baby greens

4 very thin, large slices Black Forest ham

1. Preheat the grill.
2. Place the figs, cut side up, on a plate. Brush the tops lightly with olive oil; add a sprinkling of rosemary leaves to each.
3. Place the figs, cut side down, on the hot grate and grill just until warmed, 1 to 2 minutes. One at a time remove the figs from the grill, turn them cut side up, and top with a curl of cheese. Place the figs back on the grill, cheese side up. Grill, covered, just until the cheese is warmed, 1 to 2 minutes. (If using a broiler, heat the figs cut side up just until they are warmed; then add the cheese and broil 1 minute more. Do not turn broiled figs over.)
4. Whisk the 3 tablespoons olive oil, the vinegar, a grinding of black pepper, and the salt in a large bowl. Add the salad greens and toss to coat. Divide among 4 salad plates. Tuck 2 fig halves into each salad, and drape a slice of ham over the salad.

variation: Substitute Parmigiano-Reggiano for the Comté cheese and prosciutto di Parma for the ham.

fresh fig and green tomato salad with basil

*W*hen I mentioned that I was thinking of combining summer tomatoes and figs in a salad, a chef friend suggested that I pair the figs with the most acidic tomatoes I could find. He was right. I use Green Zebra (called "zebra" because they are striped) tomatoes, an heirloom variety now popular in many produce stores and farmers' markets. This salad is perfect for a summer meal when simple is best and fresh figs, heirloom tomatoes, and fresh basil are plentiful. For an interesting variation, add some fresh tender raw corn kernels to the mix.

4 Green Zebra tomatoes (about 1 pound), cored and cut into ½-inch wedges

4 large firm ripe figs, any variety, stems trimmed, cut into ½-inch wedges

½ cup hand-torn fresh basil leaves (½-inch pieces)

½ cup paper-thin slivers of red onion

½ cup (approximately) fresh corn kernels (cut from 1 ear), optional

Kosher salt and freshly ground black pepper

3 tablespoons extra virgin olive oil

1 tablespoon aged red wine vinegar

1. Combine the tomatoes, figs, basil, and onion in a serving bowl. Add the corn, if using. Sprinkle with salt and a grinding of black pepper.
2. Drizzle the salad with the olive oil, and splash the vinegar over the top. Very gently fold together, and serve at room temperature.

grilled fresh fig salad with cantaloupe, fennel, arugula, and walnuts

makes 4 servings

Perfectly ripened cantaloupe and figs, both in season at the same time, share the same sensually soft texture. The different flavor notes in this recipe—especially the sweetness of the fruit and honey, the saltiness of the nuts, and the acidity in the dressing—play off each other exceptionally well. Serve this as a first course, solo or paired with a wedge of mild creamy Saga blue or Cambozola.

❧

1 cup walnuts

4 tablespoons extra virgin olive oil

2 tablespoons honey

Kosher salt

½ fennel bulb (about 6 ounces)

4 to 6 large firm ripe figs, any variety, stems trimmed, halved lengthwise

2 tablespoons fresh lemon juice

1 teaspoon fig balsamic or other balsamic vinegar

Freshly ground black pepper

2 bunches arugula, stems trimmed (about 4 cups packed)

12 thin slices or wedges of peeled and seeded ripe cantaloupe

❧

1. Preheat the oven to 350°F.

2. Spread the walnuts in a baking pan; drizzle with 1 tablespoon each of the oil and the honey; sprinkle with salt. Roast, stirring once or twice, until golden, about 15 minutes. Remove from the oven and allow to cool.

3. Place the fennel bulb, cut side down, on a cutting board and cut into thin half-circles. There should be about 1 cup. Place the slices in a bowl of iced water and let stand for about 20 minutes; then drain well and pat dry.

4. Preheat the grill or broiler.

5. Arrange the figs, cut side up, on a plate. Stir the remaining 1 tablespoon honey and 1 tablespoon of the lemon juice together until blended. Drizzle this over the figs. Place the figs, cut side up, on a grill or under the broiler. Grill or broil until lightly browned and softened from the heat, 1 to 2 minutes. Do not turn.

6. In a large bowl combine the remaining 3 tablespoons olive oil, the remaining 1 tablespoon lemon juice, and the balsamic vinegar, ½ teaspoon salt, and a grinding of black pepper. Whisk until blended. Add the arugula, cantaloupe, and fennel; toss to coat.

7. Distribute the salad among 4 plates, dividing the ingredients evenly. Place 2 fig halves on each plate and sprinkle with the roasted walnuts. Serve at once.

fresh fig and frisée salad with goat cheese and bacon

makes 4 servings

*F*risée is a tender, pale yellow, curly-leafed type of chicory that comes in clusters. If it's not available, the tender center of a head of chicory, also known as curly endive, can be substituted. Members of the endive family all have a pleasant, slightly bitter taste and a crisp texture that pairs well with the soft sweetness of fresh figs. This is a loose adaptation of the classic French salad made with a poached egg and thick chunks of bacon; here the figs are substituted for the eggs.

❧

4 slices thick-cut bacon

4 to 6 large firm ripe figs, any variety, stems trimmed, quartered

6 tablespoons extra virgin olive oil

2 tablespoons sherry vinegar or aged red wine vinegar

¾ teaspoon Dijon mustard

½ teaspoon kosher salt

¼ teaspoon minced garlic

8 ounces frisée or tender white leaves of chicory, trimmed, torn into small pieces
(4 to 6 cups packed)

1 tablespoon snipped fresh chives

4 ounces fresh goat cheese, well chilled, crumbled or diced

Freshly ground black pepper

❧

1. Cook the bacon in a medium skillet over medium-low heat, turning it occasionally, until browned and crisp. Drain on a paper towel. Cut into ¼-inch-wide pieces.
2. Place the figs in a small bowl and set it aside.
3. Whisk the oil, vinegar, mustard, salt, and garlic together in a large bowl until creamy. Measure out 1 tablespoon and drizzle it over the figs; toss to coat. Add the frisée and chives to the remaining dressing, and toss to coat.
4. Divide the salad among 4 salad plates. Top with the figs, and sprinkle the goat cheese over the salads. Add a grinding of pepper to each salad. Top with the bacon. Drizzle any dressing left in the small bowl on top of the salads. Serve at room temperature.

apple salad with dried figs, parmigiano-reggiano, and walnuts

makes 4 servings

*A*pples *and coarse pieces of Parmigiano-Reggiano are a favorite snack, as are dried figs and walnuts. One day, in need of a quick lunch, I combined these four ingredients, and before I knew it, I had a salad. Make this salad in midwinter when lettuces look pale and wan. Use the crispest apples you can fine. I like Fuji or Granny Smith apples, but any crunchy, slightly tart apple will do.*

3 tablespoons extra virgin olive oil

2 tablespoons fresh lemon juice

1 tablespoon honey

Kosher salt and freshly ground black pepper

2 large, crisp, tart apples, quartered, peeled, cored, cut into ¼-inch dice

8 ounces moist dried Calimyrna figs, stems trimmed, cut into ¼-inch dice (about 1¼ cups)

1 cup diced (¼-inch) celery

¼ cup diced (¼-inch) Parmigiano-Reggiano cheese

¼ cup broken walnuts

¼ cup diced (¼-inch) red onion

2 tablespoons chopped pale yellow celery leaves

Crisp radicchio, watercress sprigs, or interior pale green chicory leaves

1. Combine the olive oil, lemon juice, honey, a pinch of salt, and a grinding of black pepper in a serving bowl; whisk to blend.
2. Add the apples, figs, celery, Parmigiano-Reggiano, walnuts, red onion, and celery leaves. Toss to blend.
3. To serve, place the radicchio, several sprigs of watercress, or chicory leaves on 4 salad plates, and add a large mounded spoonful of the salad to each one. Serve at once. This is best eaten at room temperature.

the classic fig drizzle

Jazz up halved fresh figs, either plain or stuffed with cheese, with a drizzle of this amazing glaze of reduced balsamic vinegar, red wine, honey, and rosemary. Use for snacks, salads, or desserts. The recipe is adapted from Lesley Stiles, chef, caterer, and director of Contra Costa certified farmers' markets. We both agree that this recipe is a great way to use up bottles of not very good supermarket balsamic vinegar.

❧

8 cups inexpensive balsamic vinegar

2 cups red wine

½ cup honey

two 3-inch stems fresh rosemary

❧

Combine the balsamic vinegar, red wine, honey, and rosemary in a large saucepan and heat to boiling. Cook, uncovered, over medium heat, stirring occasionally, until the mixture has cooked down to about 3 cups, 50 to 60 minutes. Allow to cool. Store in the refrigerator in a recycled vinegar bottle for easy pouring or in a plastic squeeze bottle for drizzling. Keeps indefinitely.

fig vinegar

*F*ruit-flavored vinegars are expensive to buy and easy to make. This version of fig vinegar is sweet enough to use on salads without adding olive oil.

❧

3 cups red wine vinegar

6 ounces dried Calimyrna or Black Mission figs, stems trimmed, cut up (about 1 cup packed)

¼ cup sugar

1 cinnamon stick

❧

1. Combine the vinegar, figs, sugar, and cinnamon stick in a medium saucepan and heat to a boil. Reduce the heat to low and cook, covered, 5 minutes. Let stand 24 hours.
2. Strain the vinegar, pressing down on the figs to extract their flavor. Reserve half of the figs; discard the remaining and the cinnamon stick.
3. Puree the vinegar and the reserved figs in a food processor.
4. Line the strainer with a doubled layer of dampened cheesecloth and set it over a bowl. Pour the pureed vinegar mixture into the cheesecloth-lined strainer; press down on the solids; drain for 30 minutes. Transfer the strained vinegar to a jar and store in a cool dark place or in the refrigerator.

main courses

and

side dishes

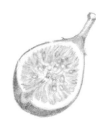

braised chicken with fennel and dried figs

makes 4 servings

*D*ried figs and fennel, both important ingredients in the cooking of the eastern Mediterranean region, are often paired in sweets like candies and cakes, but I take liberty with the combination and pair them in a simple braise of chicken. As they slowly cook, the dried figs absorb the heady chicken and fennel-laced broth, becoming juicy and succulent.

❧

1 fennel bulb (about 12 ounces)

8 ounces dried Calimyrna figs (12 to 14 figs), stems trimmed

1 whole chicken (about 3½ pounds), cut into 8 pieces, excess fat and skin trimmed

Kosher salt and freshly ground black pepper

1 tablespoon unsalted butter

1 tablespoon extra virgin olive oil

2 medium or 1 large leek, roots and green tops trimmed, soaked in warm water, rinsed thoroughly, cut into 1-inch lengths

2 medium carrots, cut into 1-inch lengths

1 teaspoon fennel seeds, bruised with a mortar and pestle or the side of a heavy knife

1 garlic clove, minced

1 cup chicken broth

1 cup dry white wine

❧

1. Trim the stem end and the dark green tops from the fennel; reserve a few fronds for garnish. Cut the fennel bulb lengthwise into quarters; then cut across into 1-inch pieces. Chill in a bowl of iced water for 20 minutes; drain.

2. Meanwhile, bring a small pan of water to a boil. Place the figs in a small bowl and cover with boiling water; let stand for 10 minutes. Drain, and cut the figs in half.

3. Sprinkle the chicken pieces with salt and pepper. Heat the butter and olive oil in a large deep skillet until sizzling. Add the chicken, a few pieces at a time, and cook until lightly browned, about 5 minutes per side. As it browns, transfer the chicken to a side dish. Leave a thin film of oil in the bottom of the pan: discard any remaining oil.

4. Add the fennel, leeks, and carrots to the pan. Cook, stirring, until the vegetables have softened, about 5 minutes. Add the figs and fennel seeds to the pan. Cook, stirring, until the cut sides of the figs are lightly browned, about 5 minutes. Add the garlic and cook, stirring, for 1 minute.

5. Add the chicken broth and the wine and heat to a boil. Boil, uncovered, over high heat until the liquid is reduced by half, about 5 minutes. Add the cooked chicken and any accumulated juices to the pan. Cover and cook over medium-low heat until the chicken juices run clear when the flesh is pierced with a fork, about 15 minutes.

6. Using a slotted spoon, transfer the chicken, vegetables, and figs to a warmed serving platter; cover to keep warm. Boil the juices over high heat until reduced and slightly thickened, 1 to 2 minutes. Pour the juices over the chicken; garnish with the reserved fennel fronds, and serve.

chicken breasts stuffed with fresh figs and goat cheese

makes 4 servings

*T*his elegant recipe–good enough for entertaining–goes together in a few minutes and cooks in less than half an hour. Serve it with a side dish of freshly cooked green beans seasoned with olive oil, chopped fresh mint, and salt.

✤

4 large boneless and skinless chicken breast halves, fillets removed (see Note)

1 tablespoon fresh thyme leaves

Kosher salt and freshly ground black pepper

1 cup diced fresh green or black figs (about 6 figs)

½ cup crumbled well-chilled goat cheese

2 tablespoons extra virgin olive oil

½ teaspoon minced garlic

4 slices (about ⅛ inch thick) pancetta or bacon

½ cup dry white wine

✤

1. Preheat the oven to 400°F.
2. Place the chicken breasts, smooth side up, on a work surface with the thickest portion to your right. Butterfly the breast by cutting through the thick side toward the tapered side so that you can open the breast like a book. Sprinkle the butterflied chicken breasts inside and out with ½ tablespoon of the thyme leaves, a pinch of salt, and a grinding of pepper.
3. In a small bowl combine the remaining ½ tablespoon thyme, the figs, the goat cheese, 1

tablespoon of the olive oil, the garlic, ½ teaspoon salt, and a grinding of black pepper. Toss to combine. Spoon the stuffing onto one side of each chicken breast, dividing it evenly. Close the chicken over the stuffing. Wrap a slice of pancetta around each chicken breast. Hold the breast closed and the pancetta in place with a toothpick or a small metal skewer.

4. Oil a large (about 13 × 9-inch) shallow flameproof baking pan with the remaining 1 tablespoon olive oil. Place the chicken breasts in the pan and roast in the oven for 10 minutes. Turn and roast the other side until cooked through, about 10 minutes.

5. Remove the pan from the oven; transfer the chicken to a serving platter and cover with foil. Add the wine to the pan and heat to a boil over high heat, scraping up the browned bits and reducing the wine to a syrup, about 5 minutes. Drizzle the wine over the chicken, and serve.

note: The fillet is the long slender piece attached to the bottom side of each breast half. They are sometimes removed from the chicken breasts and sold separately as "chicken tenders." Pull them off and reserve them for another use, such as in stir-fries or soup.

curried chicken thighs with dried figs and tomatoes

*S*picy from the subtle heat of the curry powder and rich from the taste of the dried figs, sweet potatoes, and winter squash, this is a perfect one-pot dinner for a winter night. The chicken thighs—the most flavorful part of the chicken, as far as I'm concerned—add richness and body to this stewlike dish. Serve a leafy green, such as broccoli rabe or braised collards or kale, alongside.

❦

2 teaspoons ground cumin

1 teaspoon dried thyme

Kosher salt and freshly ground black pepper

8 skinless and boneless chicken thighs

2 tablespoons extra virgin olive oil

2 large onions, chopped (about 2 cups)

2 garlic cloves, minced

2½ teaspoons Madras-style curry powder

1½ cups cut-up (½-inch cubes) peeled kabocha, butternut,
or other deep orange winter squash (about 12 ounces)

1½ cups cut-up (½-inch cubes) peeled sweet potatoes (about 12 ounces)

8 ounces dried Calimyrna or Black Mission figs (12 to 14 figs), stems trimmed

One 28-ounce can diced tomatoes with juices

1 whole clove

❦

1. Combine the cumin, thyme, ½ teaspoon salt, and a grinding of black pepper in a small bowl. Sprinkle the chicken with the spice mixture. Heat a large deep, preferably nonstick, skillet or wide saucepan over medium heat; add the olive oil.

2. Add the chicken, a few pieces at a time, to the hot oil and cook until lightly browned, about 2 minutes per side. As the chicken browns, transfer it to a side dish.

3. Add the onions to the skillet and cook until golden, 5 to 8 minutes. Add the garlic and curry powder, and stir for 1 minute.

4. Return the chicken and any accumulated juices to the skillet. Scatter the squash, sweet potatoes, and figs over the chicken. Add the tomatoes and clove.

5. Reduce the heat to medium-low. Cook, covered, until the chicken and vegetables are tender, 25 to 30 minutes. Uncover and simmer until the juices are slightly reduced, about 5 minutes. Taste and add salt and pepper if needed. Serve piping hot.

chicken, couscous, and dried fig salad with toasted almonds

makes 6 servings as a main-course salad

Instant couscous "cooks" by soaking in boiling water for 10 to 15 minutes, which allows just enough time to chop and assemble the other ingredients for this salad. The combination of couscous, fresh mint, and dill topped with a lemony dressing gives the salad a Middle Eastern flavor, with the figs adding just the right hint of sweetness and crunch to the mix.

❧

1½ cups couscous

2½ cups boiling water

Kosher salt

½ cup extra virgin olive oil

⅓ cup fresh lemon juice

1 garlic clove, minced

1 teaspoon grated lemon zest

Freshly ground black pepper

2 cups shredded cooked chicken (skinless and boneless)

1 romaine lettuce heart, cut into thin crosswise slices (about 2 cups)

8 ounces moist dried Calimyrna figs, stems trimmed, cut into ½-inch pieces (about 1¼ cups)

1 cup diced (¼-inch) firm ripe plum tomatoes, plus 2 tomatoes, trimmed and quartered

½ cup diced (¼-inch) cucumber, plus 6 slices

½ cup lightly packed chopped flat-leaf parsley leaves

½ cup lightly packed chopped fresh mint leaves

¼ cup chopped fresh dill

½ cup sliced natural (unskinned) almonds

❧

1. Place the couscous in a bowl. Add the boiling water and ½ teaspoon salt, and stir once. Cover tightly and let stand until water is absorbed and couscous is tender, 10 to 15 minutes.

2. Whisk the olive oil, lemon juice, garlic, lemon zest, ½ teaspoon salt, and black pepper in a small bowl until blended.

3. When the couscous has absorbed all the liquid, turn the bowl over onto a large deep platter and break the couscous apart with a chopstick or the handle of a wooden spoon. Allow it to cool slightly.

4. Add the chicken, romaine, figs, the diced tomatoes, diced cucumber, parsley, mint, and dill to the couscous. Top with the dressing. Gently toss the ingredients together, using your fingertips to separate the grains of couscous if necessary, until combined.

5. Clean the rim of the platter if necessary, and arrange the tomato wedges and cucumber slices around the edges of the salad. Heat the almonds in a small skillet over medium-low heat, stirring, until toasted, about 5 minutes. Sprinkle the almonds on top, and serve at room temperature. (If you are making the salad ahead and refrigerating it, allow it to warm up to room temperature before serving. Taste and add more oil and lemon juice if needed.)

honey-glazed game hens with lemon and fresh figs

*F*or moist, succulent poultry, soak it in salted water for several hours be-fore cooking (this is called brining). Some cooks add spices, garlic, herbs, and other ingredients to their brine, but I prefer to use kosher salt only.

❧

4 Rock Cornish game hens

Kosher salt

Freshly ground black pepper

2 tablespoons extra virgin olive oil

2 tablespoons finely chopped garlic

8 fresh basil leaves

3 tablespoons fresh lemon juice

3 tablespoons honey

1 lemon, cut into ¼-inch-thick slices, seeds removed

8 large firm ripe figs, any variety, stems trimmed, halved lengthwise

❧

1. Rinse the hens well with cold water, and drain. Use kitchen shears to cut along one side of the backbone of each hen. Open the hens flat and cut in half through the breastbone. Rinse again. Place the halved hens in a large bowl and add 3 tablespoons salt. Add enough water to generously cover the hens. Cover tightly and refrigerate for 2 to 4 hours. Drain, rinse, and pat dry before roasting.

2. Preheat the oven to 400°F.

3. Rub the hens with salt and pepper. Place them, skin side up, in a large sheet pan or roasting pan. (Do not crowd them; use two pans if necessary.)

4. Drizzle the hens with the olive oil, rubbing to coat them evenly. Tuck ¾ teaspoon of the garlic and a whole basil leaf under the breast skin of each half. Turn the hens skin side down. Stir the lemon juice and honey together. Brush the hens lightly with about 2 tablespoons of this basting mixture. Top with the lemon slices.

5. Roast for 30 minutes. Remove the pan from the oven and turn the hens skin side up. Brush with the pan juices and then with about 2 tablespoons more of the basting mixture. Roast for 15 minutes. Baste with the remaining honey-lemon mixture. Roast until the hens are golden brown, about 10 minutes more.

6. Transfer the hens to a serving dish and cover with foil. Arrange the figs in the pan, cut side down. Spoon the pan juices over the figs, and sprinkle the figs with a pinch of salt and a grinding of black pepper. Return the pan to the oven and roast the figs until the cut sides are caramelized, about 10 minutes.

7. Garnish the hens with the lemon slices and caramelized figs. Spoon the pan juices over the hens, and serve.

fig heaven

pan-braised duck legs with marsala and fresh fig jam

makes 4 servings

*D*uck parts are a convenience for those of us who like duck but don't always feel up to messing with a whole bird. Duck legs are less expensive than breasts, and just as good. They adapt perfectly to this slow braise with figs and Marsala, a rich fortified Sicilian wine. The figs, cooked into a chunky jam, are a picture to behold when spooned over the golden duck legs. For a side dish, serve potatoes that have been roasted to a golden crisp in the rendered duck fat or in olive oil.

❧

6 duck legs (about 10 ounces each), halved at the joint

Kosher salt and freshly ground black pepper

6 large shallots, peeled and separated into lobes

1¼ cups sweet (fine) Marsala

8 firm ripe green or black figs, stems trimmed, quartered lengthwise

1 tablespoon sugar

1 tablespoon fresh lemon juice

1 tablespoon fresh thyme leaves

❧

1. Trim off and discard all visible fat from the duck, reserving a 1-inch piece. Sprinkle the legs evenly with salt and freshly ground black pepper.

2. Place the reserved piece of duck fat in a large deep skillet or sauté pan, and cook over medium heat until the fat is rendered and the skillet is coated with a thin film of fat; discard

the solid piece of fat. Add the duck legs, skin side down, and cook, uncovered, over medium-low heat until the skin is well browned and plenty of fat has been rendered, about 20 minutes. Transfer the duck to a side dish.

3. Spoon off all but 1 tablespoon of the fat. (Reserve the fat for another use; it is delicious for roasted potatoes.)

4. Add the shallots to the skillet and cook, turning, until lightly browned, about 5 minutes. Add 1 cup of the Marsala and boil over medium-high heat, scraping the browned bits from the bottom of the pan, until the wine is reduced by half, about 5 minutes.

5. Return the duck to the skillet and cook slowly, covered, over low heat until the meat is fork-tender, 35 to 40 minutes. While it is cooking, check the moisture level in the pan often and add water, ¼ cup at a time, as needed to keep the duck moist.

6. Transfer the duck and shallots to a serving platter and cover with foil. Boil off any juices that might be left in the pan. Add the remaining ¼ cup Marsala and the figs to the pan. Sprinkle with the sugar. Cook, stirring, until the liquid is reduced, the sugar caramelized, and the figs softened and cooked into a chunky jam, about 5 minutes. Stir the lemon juice into the figs.

7. Spoon the figs over the duck and shallots; garnish with the thyme. Serve at once.

fig heaven

salmon and potatoes roasted on fig leaves with fresh fig salad

makes 4 servings

*B*est known as the lingerie of biblical times, fig leaves are truly beautiful. They are a vibrant green color, larger than an adult hand, with a
dull matte sheen and a coarse texture. Throughout the Mediterranean region,
where figs flourish, the leaves are used in cooking. As the fig leaf roasts, its
edges curl and the leaf becomes crisp. The oils in the leaf impart a subtle
herbaceous flavor to the food resting on it. In the following recipe it's the potatoes that absorb the unique flavor from the leaf. This recipe is an adaptation of one generously shared by Staffan Terje, the executive chef at Scala's
Bistro, one of my favorite restaurants in San Francisco. If you don't have access to fig leaves, roast the salmon directly on the potatoes.

❧

1 pound Yukon Gold potatoes, peeled and cut into ⅛-inch-thick slices

1 tablespoon fresh thyme or lemon thyme leaves, plus 4 small sprigs

Kosher salt and freshly ground black pepper

6 tablespoons extra virgin olive oil

4 large or 8 medium-sized fig leaves

4 large firm ripe figs, any variety, stems trimmed

1 tablespoon minced red onion

1 tablespoon fresh lime juice

½ teaspoon grated lime zest

4 boneless and skinless salmon fillets (6 to 8 ounces each)

❧

1. Place ½ cup water in a 10-inch nonstick skillet. Arrange a layer of potato slices, slightly overlapping, on the bottom of the pan; sprinkle with ½ teaspoon of the thyme, a pinch of salt, and a grinding of black pepper; drizzle with 2 tablespoons of the olive oil. Repeat with the remaining potatoes, ½ teaspoon thyme, salt, pepper, and 2 tablespoons olive oil. Cover and cook over medium-high heat until sizzling. Reduce the heat to medium-low and cook, shaking the pan occasionally, until the potatoes are very tender, about 15 minutes. Uncover and let stand off the heat until slightly cooled.

2. Meanwhile, preheat the oven to 500°F. Lightly oil a large rimmed sheet pan. Arrange the fig leaves on the pan. If using smaller leaves, place 2 leaves, stem ends overlapping, together. Set pan aside.

3. Prepare the fig salad: Using a sharp knife, carefully cut the figs into ½-inch-thick wedges. Cut each wedge across into 3 or more ½-inch pieces. Place them in a medium bowl. Add the red onion, lime juice, lime zest, a sprinkling of salt, and a grinding of black pepper; drizzle with the remaining 2 tablespoons olive oil. Gently fold to combine. Set aside at room temperature until ready to serve.

4. Just before serving, carefully arrange a portion of the potatoes in a thick layer in the center of each fig leaf. Top each layer of potatoes with a salmon fillet. (If not using fig leaves, spread the potatoes in a shallow baking dish and place the salmon on top.) Sprinkle the salmon with salt, a grinding of black pepper, and the remaining thyme leaves. Roast until the salmon is cooked through and the fig leaves are crisp and curled on the edges, 12 to 15 minutes, depending on the thickness of the salmon.

5. Slide a wide spatula under each fig leaf and transfer the leaf, salmon, and potatoes to a dinner plate. Carefully arrange a spoonful of the fig salad on top of each piece of salmon. Garnish each serving with a sprig of fresh thyme.

oven-roasted halibut with onions, orange, and fresh or dried figs

makes 4 servings

*T*hick pieces of fresh fish fillet retain their moisture and flavor if oven-roasted at a high temperature for a short time. Escolar, salmon, halibut, cod, and moonfish (opah) all work with this method. I prefer fresh green figs (Calimyrna, Kadota, Desert King) in this recipe; their color is stunning next to the red onions. But if you are using white or yellow onions, use Black Mission figs. Chopped steamed broccoli, or another bitter green vegetable, makes an excellent accompaniment.

❧

2 medium red onions (about 1 pound), cut into ½-inch wedges

2 strips orange zest, each about ½ × 2 inches, cut into long thin slivers

2 tablespoons extra virgin olive oil

Kosher salt and freshly ground black pepper

8 firm ripe green figs, stems trimmed, halved lengthwise

1 teaspoon dried oregano or 1 tablespoon minced fresh oregano

4 portions skinless and boneless halibut fillets or steaks, about ¾ inch thick,
6 to 8 ounces each

¼ cup fresh orange juice

❧

1. Preheat the oven to 400°F.
2. Spread the onions and orange zest in a large (13 × 9-inch) roasting pan; drizzle with the olive oil; season with salt and a grinding of black pepper. Roast for 15 minutes, stirring

once. Add the figs (if using dried, see the Variation below) and half of the oregano. Roast until the onions begin to brown at the edges, about 10 minutes. Remove the pan from the oven. Increase the oven temperature to 450°F.

3. Push the onions and figs to the side in the pan and add the halibut. Drizzle the orange juice over the fish. Sprinkle with the remaining oregano and salt and pepper to taste. Spoon some of the onions on top of the halibut. Return the pan to the oven and roast until the fish is cooked through, 10 to 12 minutes.

4. Serve at once, with the roasted onions and figs spooned over the fish.

variation with dried figs: Trim off the stems of 8 dried Calimyrna or Black Mission figs. Combine the figs and 1 cup water in a small saucepan and heat to a boil. Cook, covered, over low heat until the figs are plumped and tender and most of the water has been absorbed, 20 to 25 minutes. Cool; then drain and cut the figs in half. The figs can be prepared 2 or 3 days ahead and refrigerated, tightly covered, until ready to use.

soy-glazed tuna with fresh fig, peach, and sesame salsa

makes 4 servings

The flavors in this fresh fig and peach salsa are especially fresh and bright-tasting. The toasted sesame oil and sesame seeds pair up well with the soy-glazed tuna, but don't hesitate to try the salsa with soy-glazed salmon or pork tenderloins. Use firm ripe figs that will retain their shape when they are diced for the salsa.

❧

4 tablespoons soy sauce

4 teaspoons toasted sesame oil

1 teaspoon grated fresh ginger

1 teaspoon minced garlic

1½ pounds boneless and skinless tuna steaks or boneless and skinless salmon fillets, ¾ to 1 inch thick (see Note)

4 to 5 large firm ripe green or black figs, stems trimmed, cut into ¼-inch dice

½ cup peeled and diced (¼-inch) ripe peach or nectarine

¼ cup diced (⅛-inch) seedless cucumber

1 tablespoon thinly sliced scallion (white and green parts)

2 teaspoons brown (unhulled) sesame seeds

1 teaspoon minced jalapeño, or to taste

1 tablespoon fresh lime juice

½ teaspoon kosher salt

❧

1. Combine the soy sauce, 2 teaspoons of the sesame oil, the ginger, and the garlic in a bowl, and stir to blend. Place the tuna in a large heavy food storage bag, and add the marinade. Seal the bag and refrigerate while preparing the salsa.

2. Combine the figs, peach, cucumber, scallion, sesame seeds, jalapeño, lime juice, salt, and the remaining 2 teaspoons sesame oil in a medium bowl. Gently fold just to blend. Refrigerate the salsa until ready to serve.

3. Preheat the grill or place a large heavy nonstick skillet on high heat until it is hot enough to sizzle and evaporate a drop of water. Lift the tuna from the marinade, reserving the marinade. Grill the tuna over high heat for 2 to 3 minutes per side for rare, 3 to 4 minutes per side for medium-rare. The timing will depend on the heat intensity of the grill. Brush some of the marinade on the tuna while it is grilling. To cook the tuna in a skillet, sear it for 2 minutes on one side; turn and sear 2 minutes more; drizzle with about 1 tablespoon of the marinade and sear 1 minute more on each side for rare. For medium-rare, cook 1 minute more on each side.

4. Serve immediately, with the salsa spooned over the tuna.

note: If you are using salmon, grill or broil the salmon for 3 to 4 minutes per side, brushing the tops with the reserved marinade while cooking. If using pork tenderloin, you will need 1 tenderloin for 2 to 3 servings. Follow the same procedure for marinating, but cook the tenderloin 5 to 8 minutes per side, depending on its thickness. Cut the tenderloin in 1/4-inch diagonal slices and spoon the salsa on top.

lamb stew with artichokes and dried figs

*L*amb, artichokes, and dried figs remind me of the Mediterranean, my favorite place to travel and to eat. This recipe is a compendium of many of the flavors I love about this beautiful region, but its authenticity comes only from my imagination. Serve the stew with steaming couscous, rice, or bulgur.

❧

1 to 1½ pounds boneless lamb stew meat or sirloin (cut from the leg), cut into ½ × 1-inch pieces

Kosher salt and freshly ground black pepper

¼ cup all-purpose flour

4 tablespoons extra virgin olive oil

2 medium onions, cut into ½-inch wedges (about 2 cups)

½ cup sliced carrot (¼-inch rounds)

2 garlic cloves, bruised with the side of a heavy knife

1 teaspoon ground cumin

½ cup dry white or red wine

One 28-ounce can plum tomatoes with juice, coarsely cut into 1-inch pieces

8 ounces dried Calimyrna or Black Mission figs (12 to 14 figs), stems trimmed

2 strips orange zest, each about ½ × 2 inches

One 3-inch cinnamon stick

One 12-ounce bag or 10-ounce package frozen artichoke hearts, thawed and blotted dry

2 tablespoons coarsely chopped fresh dill

2 tablespoons coarsely chopped fresh mint

❧

1. Sprinkle the lamb with salt and pepper. Place the flour in a plastic bag, add a few pieces of the lamb, and shake to coat. Remove and shake off the excess flour. Repeat with the remaining lamb.

2. Heat a deep skillet or sauté pan with a tight-fitting lid over medium heat; add 2 tablespoons of the olive oil.

3. Add half of the lamb to the hot oil and cook until evenly browned, about 15 minutes. Transfer the lamb to a side dish. Repeat with the remaining lamb.

4. Add another tablespoon of oil to the pan, if needed. Add the onions and carrots to the hot oil and cook, stirring, until the onions are golden, about 10 minutes. Add the garlic and cumin and cook for 1 minute. Transfer the vegetables to the side dish with the lamb.

5. Add the wine and boil over high heat until reduced by half. Then add the tomatoes, figs, 1 strip of the orange zest, and the cinnamon stick; heat to a boil. Return the lamb and any accumulated juices to the skillet. Cook, covered, over medium-low heat until the lamb is very tender, about 1½ hours.

6. Meanwhile, heat the remaining 1 tablespoon olive oil in a large skillet and cook the artichoke hearts, turning them with a spatula, until golden brown, about 15 minutes.

7. About 15 minutes before the lamb is cooked, stir the artichoke hearts into the stew. Taste and add salt and pepper if needed.

8. Finely chop the dill, mint, and reserved orange zest together. Sprinkle this over the stew, and serve.

fresh fig–stuffed pork loin with fennel and onions

makes 6 to 8 servings

*T*his dish makes a dramatic presentation for a celebratory meal. The pork is stuffed with a row of figs arranged so that when the roast is cut, there is a nice round of fresh fig in each slice. The white wine used to deglaze the roasting pan combines with the juices to make a light sauce for the meat.

❧

1 fennel bulb (about 12 ounces)

1 boneless pork loin (3 to 4 pounds), untied (see Note)

4 garlic cloves, crushed with the side of a heavy knife

1 tablespoon fennel seeds, crushed with a mortar and pestle
or the side of a heavy knife

1 tablespoon minced fresh rosemary

Kosher salt and freshly ground black pepper

12 to 14 firm ripe green figs, stems trimmed

1 large or 2 medium onions, cut into ½-inch wedges

2 tablespoons extra virgin olive oil

1 cup fruity white wine, such as Riesling or Pinot Gris

❧

1. Trim the base of the fennel bulb. Trim off the tops and reserve enough of the tender fronds to make ½ cup chopped; reserve for later. Cut the bulb in half lengthwise; place the halves, cut side down, on a cutting board and cut each one into 3 lengthwise wedges. Soak the fennel wedges in a bowl of iced water for 20 minutes; drain.

2. Preheat the oven to 400°F.

3. Cut eight 18-inch lengths of cotton string. With a thin sharp knife, cut the pork loin lengthwise down the center, about three-quarters of the way through, so it can be opened like a book.

4. Combine the chopped fennel fronds, garlic, fennel seeds, rosemary, 1 teaspoon salt, and ¼ teaspoon black pepper and finely chop together. Rub half of this garlic mixture into the opened pork. Arrange 6 to 8 of the figs on their sides, close together, in a single row down the center of the bottom portion of the pork. (Reserve the remaining figs.) Fold the top portion of the pork over the bottom. Slide the strings under the pork, evenly spaced, and tie them firmly but not too tightly. If any figs pop out, poke them back.

5. Rub the outside of the pork thoroughly with the remaining garlic mixture. Place the pork in a roasting pan, and scatter the fennel and onions around it. Drizzle the olive oil over the meat and vegetables. Roast for 30 minutes.

6. Carefully turn the roast over. Turn the fennel and rearrange the onions. Halve the remaining figs and add them to the pan. Sprinkle the vegetables and figs with salt and pepper. Roast until a meat thermometer inserted in the pork registers a temperature of 135°F, about 30 minutes. Remove the pork from the pan to a carving board and tent it with foil to keep it warm. Let it stand for 10 minutes before carving. (The internal temperature will rise as the pork rests.)

7. Transfer the figs, onions, fennel, and juices to a wide saucepan or sauté pan; keep warm over low heat. Pour the wine into the roasting pan and set the pan over low heat. Heat to a boil, using a spatula to scrape any browned bits from the bottom of the pan. Boil until the wine is reduced by almost half, about 2 minutes. Add the reduced wine to the figs and vegetables in the saucepan. Taste, and add salt and pepper if needed. Heat to a simmer.

8. Remove the strings from the pork. Carefully carve the roast into ½-inch-thick slices, being careful to include a portion of fig in the center of each slice. Arrange the slices, slightly overlapping, on a platter. Spoon the vegetables and figs around the pork, and pour the juices over the slices. Serve at once.

note: A well-trimmed boneless pork loin has had the long narrow strip of meat called the tenderloin removed. The resulting roast measures only about 3 to 4 inches in diameter and 12 or more inches long. This is the cut that is required for this roast.

dried fig and apple–stuffed pork loin with cider sauce

makes 6 to 8 servings

Apples and pork are a traditional duo, especially in the fall. In this pork loin the apple stuffing is embellished with cider-plumped dried figs, caramelized onions, and fresh sage. The pan juices are combined with additional cider and white wine for the sauce.

12 ounces large dried Calimyrna figs (12 to 14 figs), left whole with stems attached

3 cups apple cider

3 tablespoons extra virgin olive oil

2 cups cubed (½-inch) onions

2 cups cubed (½-inch) unpeeled firm cooking apples, such as Jonathan, Gravenstein, or Granny Smith (about 12 ounces)

1 tablespoon coarsely chopped garlic

1 tablespoon coarsely chopped fresh sage, plus more for garnish

Kosher salt and freshly ground black pepper

1 boneless pork loin roast (3 to 4 pounds), untied (see Note, page 84)

1 cup fruity white wine, such as Pinot Gris or Riesling

1 tablespoon fresh lemon juice, optional

1. Combine the figs and 2 cups of the apple cider in a medium saucepan and heat to a boil. Cook, covered, over low heat until the figs have softened and all but ¼ cup of the liquid has been absorbed, 20 to 25 minutes. Boil, uncovered, to reduce any excess liquid. Cool the figs in the liquid; then strain, reserving the ¼ cup of cider syrup. Set aside 8 whole figs.

Using kitchen scissors, trim the stems from the remaining figs and cut them into ½-inch pieces.

2. Heat 2 tablespoons of the olive oil in a large skillet. Add the onions and apples and cook, stirring, over medium heat until the onions are golden, about 15 minutes. Add the garlic, ½ tablespoon of the sage, and salt and pepper to taste. Cook for 1 minute. Stir in the cut-up figs. Set aside to cool.

3. Preheat the oven to 350°F.

4. Cut eight 18-inch lengths of cotton string. With a thin sharp knife, cut the pork lengthwise down the center, about three-quarters of the way through, so it can be opened like a book. Season the opened pork with a sprinkling of salt and a grinding of black pepper.

5. Spoon about half of the apple-fig mixture in a thick layer over the bottom portion of the pork, spreading it evenly. Fold the top portion of the pork over the bottom. Slide the strings under the pork, evenly spaced, and tie them firmly but not too tightly. Tuck any stuffing that escapes back into the roast. Rub the remaining ½ tablespoon sage and a generous amount of salt and pepper over the outside of the pork.

6. Heat a Dutch oven or other large, heavy ovenproof pan over medium heat until it is hot enough to sizzle and evaporate a drop of water. Add the remaining 1 tablespoon olive oil. Add the pork and sear it on all sides until golden brown, about 2 to 3 minutes per side. Remove the pan from the heat, and spoon the remaining apple-fig mixture around the pork.

7. Place the pan in the oven and roast, uncovered, for 15 minutes. Remove the pan and carefully turn the roast over. Roast until a meat thermometer inserted in the pork registers a temperature of 135°F, 10 to 15 minutes more. (The internal temperature will rise as the pork rests out of the oven.)

8. Remove the pan from the oven, transfer the roast to a cutting board, and tent it with foil to keep it warm. Spoon the apple-fig mixture into a serving dish and cover to keep it warm.

9. And the remaining 1 cup apple cider, the wine, and the reserved ¼ cup apple cider syrup to the pan. Heat to a boil, scraping the browned bits from the bottom of the pan. Boil until the mixture is reduced to about ½ cup, about 5 minutes. Taste and add lemon juice if desired, and salt and pepper if needed.

10. Cut the meat into ½-inch-thick slices and arrange them, slightly overlapping, on a warmed platter. Spoon the apple-fig mixture around the edges, and garnish with the reserved whole figs and sage leaves. Spoon the cider sauce over the meat, and serve.

Cheese-Filled Fresh Figs (page 27)

Grilled Fresh Figs on
Rosemary Skewers (page 29)

Roasted Figs with Gorgonzola and Prosciutto di Parma (page 31)

Cream Cheese, Dried Fig, and Walnut Spread with Smoked Salmon on Endive Leaves (page 22)

*Dried Fig and Apple-Stuffed
Pork Loin with Cider Sauce
(page 85)*

*Dried Fig, Orange, Fennel, and Sweet Onion
Salad with Mixed Greens (page 47)*

Braised Chicken with Fennel and Dried Figs (page 63)

Chicken Breasts Stuffed with Fresh Figs and Goat Cheese (page 65)

Salmon and Potatoes Roasted on
Fig Leaves with Fresh Fig Salad (page 75)

Oven-Roasted Halibut with Onions, Orange, and Fresh or Dried Figs (page 77)

Fettuccine with Lemon, Rosemary, and Fresh Figs (page 87)

Fresh Fig Galette (page 103)

Fresh Fig Clafouti
(page 109)

Poached Dried Figs in
Phyllo Flowers with
Spiced Syrup (page 127)

Dried Figs and Apricots
in Vanilla Wine Syrup
(page 139)

Dried Fig, Walnut,
and Chunky Chip
Sugar Cookies
(page 123)

Fresh Figs with Mascarpone
and Orange Caramel Sauce
(page 129)

fettuccine with lemon, rosemary, and fresh figs

makes 4 servings

I was first served pasta with fig sauce by chef Christopher Mariscotti at The Vineyard Restaurant, in the heart of fig country in Madera, California. It was a revelation, and I couldn't wait to interpret the chef's recipe at home. The acidity of the lemon juice and the saltiness of the Parmigiano-Reggiano balance the sweetness of the figs in this unusual pasta dish. Use firm ripe green figs because the purple skins of Black Mission figs will turn the pasta pink.

❧

Two to three 1-inch-thick slices Italian bread, crusts trimmed, torn into pieces

6 tablespoons extra virgin olive oil

2 tablespoons pignoli (pine nuts)

½ teaspoon minced garlic

1 pound fresh green figs (Calimyrna, Kadota, or Desert King), stems trimmed, cut into ½-inch-thick wedges

1 tablespoon grated lemon zest

1 teaspoon chopped fresh rosemary

Kosher salt and freshly ground black pepper

1 pound fresh fettuccine

¼ cup fresh lemon juice

2 tablespoons butter, cut into small pieces

Freshly grated Parmigiano-Reggiano cheese

❧

1. Bring a large pot of salted water to a boil.
2. While the water is heating, pulse the bread in the bowl of a food processor until it forms coarse crumbs; there should be about 1 cup.
3. Heat 2 tablespoons of the olive oil in a medium skillet. Add the crumbs and cook, stirring, over medium-low heat until they are toasted and crisp, about 5 minutes. Transfer the crumbs to a small bowl.
4. Add the pignoli to the skillet and heat, stirring constantly, over low heat until evenly golden, about 3 minutes. Add to the bowl with the toasted bread crumbs.
5. Combine the remaining 4 tablespoons olive oil and the garlic in the skillet and heat over low heat just until the garlic begins to sizzle. Add the figs and cook gently over low heat, turning carefully to coat them with the oil, for 2 minutes. Sprinkle with the lemon zest, rosemary, and salt and pepper to taste. Keep warm over very low heat.
6. Cook the fettuccine in the boiling water until al dente, 3 to 5 minutes. Ladle out ¼ cup of the pasta cooking liquid and reserve it. Drain the pasta.
7. Return the pasta to the pot, and add the reserved pasta cooking liquid and the lemon juice; toss to coat. Pour the fig mixture on top. Add the butter, and toss gently just to blend. Transfer half of the pasta to a serving platter. Sprinkle with half of the toasted crumbs and pignoli. Top with the remaining pasta, arranging some of the figs on top. Top with the remaining crumb and pignoli mixture. Cover the top generously with Parmigiano-Reggiano, and serve.

fresh fig, ricotta, and prosciutto pie

*P*art quiche and part savory custard, this crustless pie is an unusual and light main dish. Serve a salad of summer greens alongside.

❧

One 15-ounce container whole-milk or part-skim ricotta cheese

4 large eggs

¼ cup milk

2 tablespoons all-purpose flour

½ teaspoon kosher salt

⅛ teaspoon freshly ground black pepper

1 cup lightly packed fresh basil leaves

2 slices (about 2 ounces) prosciutto di Parma or other ham, minced

4 ounces fresh goat cheese, well chilled, crumbled

4 to 6 large firm ripe figs, any variety, stems trimmed, cut into ¼-inch-thick rounds

❧

1. Preheat the oven to 350°F. Butter a 9-inch pie plate.
2. Whisk the ricotta, eggs, milk, flour, salt, and pepper together in a large bowl until blended.
3. Finely chop the basil in a food processor or by hand. Add the basil, prosciutto, and half of the goat cheese to the ricotta mixture; stir until blended.
4. Pour the mixture into the prepared pie plate. Arrange the figs in concentric circles on top of the filling. Sprinkle with the remaining goat cheese.
5. Bake until the edges are lightly browned and the center is almost set, 45 to 50 minutes. Let stand 10 to 15 minutes before serving. (The center will set firm while standing.)
6. To serve, spoon onto plates. Serve either warm or at room temperature.

bulgur with walnuts and dried figs

Bulgur, with its sweet nutty flavor, goes well with dried figs and toasted walnuts. Because it is made from steamed, dried, cracked wheat berries, bulgur cooks very quickly. It is usually sold in bulk in three different textures; use a coarse-milled bulgur for pilaf. This pilaf goes especially well with lamb.

❧

3 tablespoons extra virgin olive oil

2 cups diced (¼-inch) onion

2 cups coarse bulgur

1 tablespoon minced garlic

2 teaspoons ground cumin

4 cups chicken broth, vegetable broth, or water, or part broth and part water

1 teaspoon kosher salt

8 ounces dried Calimyrna or Black Mission figs, stems trimmed,
cut into ½-inch pieces (about 1½ cups)

1 cup walnut pieces

2 tablespoons chopped fresh dill

❧

1. Combine the olive oil and onions in a large wide saucepan, deep skillet, or sauté pan. Cook, stirring, over medium-low heat, adjusting the heat as necessary, until the onions are golden, about 15 minutes.
2. Add the bulgur and stir over medium-low heat until it is toasted, about 10 minutes. Add the garlic and cook, stirring, for 2 minutes. Add the cumin and cook, stirring, until warmed, about 1 minute.

3. While the bulgur is cooking, heat the broth to a boil in a saucepan.

4. Stir the boiling broth into the bulgur. Add the salt and the figs. Cover, and cook over medium-low heat until the broth has been absorbed and the bulgur is light and fluffy, about 20 minutes. Let stand off the heat, covered, for 10 minutes before serving.

5. Meanwhile, preheat the oven to 350°F.

6. Spread the walnuts in a baking pan and heat until toasted, 10 to 15 minutes.

7. When you are ready to serve the pilaf, spoon it into a serving bowl and sprinkle with the dill and the toasted walnuts.

fresh fig risotto with prosciutto di parma

*M*y first August in California was a revelation. The nights were cool enough to sleep under a down comforter, but the markets in the bright midday sun were a kaleidoscope of fruits and vegetables unlike anything I had ever experienced. One Saturday at the market I bought figs, figs, and more figs—figs in more colors, sizes, and shapes than I had ever seen. Needless to say, when I got home with my surfeit of figs I was inspired to become inventive. This risotto is a result of that morning at the market and a fun day in the kitchen, surrounded by figs.

❧

1¼ pounds firm ripe green figs, stems trimmed

2 tablespoons unsalted butter

2 teaspoons fresh rosemary leaves

Kosher salt and freshly ground black pepper

8 cups reduced-sodium chicken broth

¼ cup minced prosciutto di Parma or pancetta

¼ cup chopped onion

1½ cups Carnaroli, Vialone Nano, Arborio, or other medium-grain risotto rice

½ cup dry white wine

¼ cup coarsely slivered Parmigiano-Reggiano cheese

12 or more thick curls of Parmigiano-Reggiano, cut with a cheese plane
or a sturdy vegetable peeler

❧

1. Select 4 of the largest, most perfect figs, and cut each one in half. Cut the remaining figs into 1/2-inch pieces and set them aside.

2. Melt 1 tablespoon of the butter in a medium skillet over low heat. Add the halved figs, cut side down, and cook over medium heat until sizzling and lightly browned, about 3 minutes. Turn them cut side up; sprinkle with the rosemary, a few grains of salt, and a grinding of black pepper. Let stand in the skillet, off the heat, until ready to serve.

3. Heat the broth to a simmer in a saucepan; keep it at a gentle simmer.

4. Melt the remaining 1 tablespoon butter in large wide saucepan or deep skillet over medium-low heat. Add the prosciutto and onion; cook, stirring, until golden, about 5 minutes. Add the rice and stir until coated, about 2 minutes. Add the wine; cook, stirring, over medium heat until it has been absorbed.

5. Add 1/2 cup of the hot chicken broth. Cook, stirring constantly, over medium heat until the broth is almost all absorbed. Add the remaining broth, 1/2 cup at a time, stirring constantly and allowing each addition to be absorbed, until the risotto is creamy and the rice is plump and tender with a slight resistance to the bite, 20 to 25 minutes. Halfway through cooking, add half of the diced figs. (If you run out of broth, finish the risotto with a little boiling water.)

6. Add the remaining diced figs and the slivered cheese. Taste the risotto, and add salt if needed. Let it stand off the heat for a few minutes before serving. Meanwhile, quickly re-heat the fig halves just until warmed.

7. Spoon the risotto into soup dishes. Place 2 fig halves on top of each serving, and top with the curls of cheese. Serve at once.

roasted root vegetables
with wine-plumped dried figs

For this grand vegetable side dish, use a variety of winter vegetables in-cluding everyday staples such as carrots, onions, and potatoes, as well as seasonal roots such as parsnips, rutabagas, and/or turnips. The slowly roasted vegetables are finished with a glaze of sweetened reduced red wine from the plumped figs. The vegetables emerge from the oven soft, fragrant, and glistening. Biting into one of the wine-plumped figs is like finding a gem nestled among the roots. Serve as a vegetarian main course accompanied by a green salad or as a side dish with roasted meat.

❧

8 ounces dried Calimyrna or Black Mission figs (12 to 14 figs), stems trimmed, halved

2 cups full-bodied red wine

1 tablespoon sugar

8 ounces parsnips, peeled, trimmed, cut into 1-inch chunks

8 ounces turnips or rutabagas, peeled, trimmed, cut into 1-inch chunks

6 ounces (about 6) shallots, peeled and separated into lobes, or boiling onions, trimmed, halved if large

6 small Yukon Gold potatoes, scrubbed, halved, or quartered if large

1 large carrot, cut into 1-inch chunks

2 tablespoons extra virgin olive oil

1 tablespoon fresh sage leaves, torn into pieces

Kosher salt and freshly ground black pepper

❧

1. Combine the figs, wine, and sugar in a medium saucepan and heat to a boil. Cook, covered, over low heat until the figs are plumped, about 25 minutes. Using a slotted spoon, remove the figs from the wine; reserve. Boil the wine, uncovered, over medium-high heat until reduced to about $1/3$ cup, about 10 minutes. Set aside.

2. Preheat the oven to 350°F.

3. Place the parsnips, turnips, shallots, potatoes, and carrots in a single layer in a large (13 × 9-inch) shallow baking dish. Add the olive oil, half of the sage leaves, and salt and pepper to taste. Toss to coat. Cover with foil and bake for 40 minutes.

4. Remove the baking dish from the oven. Using a spatula, carefully turn the vegetables. Add the figs.

5. Roast, uncovered, turning the vegetables once, until they are browned and tender, about 30 minutes. Drizzle with the reduced wine syrup during the last 10 minutes of roasting. Sprinkle with the remaining sage leaves, and serve at once.

roasted red onions and fresh figs with sherry vinegar

makes 4 to 6 servings

*T*he bright chartreuse skins of the figs are a vivid contrast to the muted purple of the caramelized red onions. Serve this as a side dish with roasted pork, chicken, or duck. The tangy vinegar balances the sweetness of the cooked onions and figs.

❦

4 medium red onions (about 1¼ pounds), cut into ¾-inch-thick wedges

2 tablespoons extra virgin olive oil

Kosher salt and freshly ground black pepper

4 to 6 firm ripe figs, preferably green, stems trimmed, halved lengthwise

1 tablespoons sherry vinegar, or more to taste

1 teaspoon snipped fresh rosemary

❦

1. Preheat the oven to 400°F.
2. Spread the onions in a large shallow (13 × 9-inch) baking dish. Drizzle with the olive oil; add ½ teaspoon salt and a generous grinding of black pepper. Roast, turning each wedge once, until the onions begin to caramelize on the edges, about 30 minutes.
3. Remove the baking dish from the oven and arrange the figs, cut sides down, between the wedges of onion. Return the dish to the oven and roast until the figs are golden on the cut sides, about 10 minutes.
4. Sprinkle with the vinegar and rosemary, and serve at once.

sweets

fresh fig smoothie

makes 1 serving

*F*resh figs make a sumptuous smoothie when combined with other fresh fruit and juice, milk, or even cold tea. To make a frosted smoothie, add a few ice cubes to the blender.

❧

1 cup fresh orange juice, lemonade, cold tea, or other beverage of choice

2 large ripe figs, stems trimmed, cubed

½ cup cut-up peeled peach, nectarine, hulled strawberries, or other fruit in season

½ cup ice cubes, optional

❧

Combine the orange juice, the figs, the cut-up fruit, and the ice cubes, if using, in a blender jar. Blend for a full minute. Pour into a tall glass and serve.

dried fig smoothie

makes 1 serving

*W*hen fresh figs are not in season, make a smoothie with dried figs. Use moist figs (plumped in boiling water for 10 minutes if necessary), cut into small pieces.

❧

1 cup fresh orange juice

1 ripe banana, sliced

½ cup low-fat milk, soy milk, or yogurt

4 moist dried Calimyrna or Black Mission figs, stems trimmed,
cut into small pieces

½ teaspoon pure vanilla extract

½ cup ice cubes, optional

❧

Combine the orange juice, banana, milk, figs, vanilla, and ice cubes, if using, in a blender jar. Blend for a full 2 minutes. Pour into a tall glass and serve.

fresh fig tart

The buttery crust for this tart couldn't be easier. It's made in the food processor and then pressed into the tart pan—no messing around with a rolling pin or worries about handling pastry in the heat of summer. Without fail, the crust is consistently tender. The fig filling is scented with orange zest and just a hint of cinnamon. Ginger-lovers might like the fig and ginger variation.

❧

1½ cups plus 2 tablespoons all-purpose flour

6 tablespoons granulated sugar

1 teaspoon ground cinnamon

¼ teaspoon salt

10 tablespoons (1 stick plus 2 tablespoons) cold unsalted butter,
cut into ½-inch pieces

1 egg yolk

1 teaspoon pure vanilla extract

2 pounds (approximately) firm ripe figs, any variety, stems trimmed

1 teaspoon grated orange zest

Confectioners' sugar

1 cup heavy cream, softly whipped, or 1 pint softened vanilla ice cream

❧

1. Preheat the oven to 400°F. Lightly butter the bottom and sides of a 9-inch loose-bottomed tart pan.
2. Combine the 1½ cups flour, 2 tablespoons of the sugar, and ½ teaspoon of the cinnamon

in the bowl of a food processor. With the processor motor running, gradually add the butter through the feed tube. Process until the mixture is crumbly.

3. Stir the egg yolk and vanilla together in a small bowl. With the motor running, gradually add the egg mixture through the feed tube. Pulse the mixture until it begins to pull together. (If the dough seems dry, sprinkle it with iced water, 1 tablespoon at a time.) The dough should be crumbly but not dry.

4. Turn the dough out directly into the prepared tart pan. Gently press it on the bottom and up the sides of the pan in a relatively even layer; the dough will have a rough surface. (The crust can be made ahead and refrigerated, covered, until ready to bake.)

5. Reserve 8 to 10 of the figs for the topping. Cut the remaining figs into ½-inch pieces. Stir the remaining 4 tablespoons sugar, remaining 2 tablespoons flour, the orange zest, and the remaining ½ teaspoon cinnamon in a large bowl until blended. Add the cut-up figs and toss gently to coat them with the sugar mixture. Spoon the filling evenly into the prepared crust; top with any sugar left in the bottom of the bowl.

6. Bake the tart for 20 minutes. Then reduce the oven temperature to 350°F and bake until the edges of the crust are golden brown and the figs are hot and bubbly, 25 to 30 minutes. Remove the tart from the oven.

7. Trim about ½ inch off the tops and bottoms of the reserved figs. Cut each fig crosswise into three or four ¼-inch-thick rounds. Carefully place the sliced figs close together on the surface of the tart, pressing them down gently into the hot fig mixture. Let the tart cool on a wire rack.

8. Before serving, remove the rim from the tart pan. Slide the tart, still on the base of the pan, onto a serving plate. Sprinkle with sieved confectioners' sugar. Cut into wedges, and serve with a spoonful of whipped cream or a scoop of softened vanilla ice cream if desired.

fresh fig tart with crystallized ginger: Omit the cinnamon from the crust and the grated orange zest and cinnamon from the filling. Add 2 tablespoons finely chopped crystallized ginger to the fig filling.

fresh fig and blueberry tart: You will need 1½ pounds of figs (any variety) and 1½ pints of blueberries. Use 1 pound of figs and 1 pint of blueberries for the filling. For the topping use 8 ounces figs and 1 cup (about ½ pint) blueberries, pressing the blueberries between the fig slices for the topping. Omit the orange zest and cinnamon.

fresh fig galette

*F*ill this free-form tart with figs or a combination of figs and peaches or nectarines—both are ripe and luscious during fig season. Use just sugar to sweeten the figs, or add minced candied ginger or a pinch of ground cinnamon. Look for coarse baker's sugar to sprinkle on the outside of the pastry before baking to give the galette a professional look.

❧

2 cups plus 3 tablespoons all-purpose flour

4 tablespoons sugar

1 teaspoon salt

11 tablespoons (1 stick plus 3 tablespoons) cold unsalted butter,
cut into ¼-inch pieces

¼ cup solid vegetable shortening

2 pounds (about 15) firm ripe green figs, stems trimmed,
cut into ½-inch-thick wedges

1 egg yolk beaten with 1 tablespoon milk

1 tablespoon coarse baker's sugar, or 1 teaspoon granulated sugar

Confectioners' sugar, optional

❧

1. Place ¼ cup water in a measuring cup and add an ice cube; set aside. Combine the 2 cups flour, 2 tablespoons of the sugar, and the salt in the bowl of a food processor; pulse to blend. Gradually add the butter, pulsing to blend. Add the shortening and pulse just until the butter and shortening have formed fine crumbs and are evenly distributed. With the motor running, drizzle the iced water, 1 tablespoon at a time, through the feed tube, puls-

ing until the mixture is dampened and comes together easily. (You might not need all of the water.)

2. Turn the pastry out onto a piece of aluminum foil, and with floured hands gather it into a ball. Flatten it to form a disc shape, wrap it in foil, and refrigerate for 1 hour.

3. When you are ready to bake the galette, preheat the oven to 400°F. Lightly butter a large cookie sheet.

4. Combine the 3 tablespoons flour and the remaining 2 tablespoons sugar in a large bowl; stir to blend. Add the figs; toss lightly to coat them with the flour mixture.

5. Roll the chilled pastry out on a lightly floured pastry cloth, using a rolling pin covered with a lightly floured stocking, to form a round about 14 inches in diameter. Using the pastry cloth, carefully invert the pastry onto the cookie sheet.

6. Spoon the fig filling onto the center of the pastry, spreading it to 3 inches from the edges. Fold the edges of the pastry in and over the filling, leaving a portion of exposed fruit in the center. Lightly brush the pastry with the egg mixture, and sprinkle it lightly with the baker's sugar.

7. Bake for 15 minutes. Reduce the oven temperature to 350°F and bake until the crust is golden and the filling is hot and bubbly, 30 to 35 minutes. Place the cookie sheet on a wire rack and allow to cool for 20 minutes. Then slide the galette off the cookie sheet onto the wire rack to finish cooling.

8. If you did not use the baker's sugar, sprinkle sieved confectioners' sugar lightly over the galette just before serving.

fresh fig and peach crumble

makes 6 to 8 servings

F or me drippy fresh peaches and sweet fresh figs represent the true tastes of summer, so it is inevitable for them to share the limelight in a dessert. You can also make this crumble with other summer fruit—figs and nectarines, figs and blueberries or raspberries, figs and apricots, or all figs with a mixture of varieties.

❧

8 tablespoons (1 stick) chilled (but not refrigerator-hard) unsalted butter, cut into big chunks

⅓ cup plus 2 tablespoons sugar

1 cup plus 2 tablespoons all-purpose flour

Pinch of salt

1 pound peaches, peeled, halved, cut into ½-inch wedges

1 pound large firm ripe figs, any variety, stems trimmed, cut into ½ inch wedges

1 tablespoon fresh lime juice

½ teaspoon ground cinnamon

Confectioners' sugar

Vanilla ice cream

❧

1. Combine the butter and ⅓ cup sugar in the large bowl of an electric mixer and beat until well combined, about 3 minutes.
2. Add the 1 cup flour and the salt, and beat on low speed just until the flour is incorporated; the mixture should be dry and crumbly. Remove the bowl from the mixer and scrape the

sweets   105 flour from the bottom and edges of the bowl, pressing it into the pastry. The pastry should still be crumbly. If your kitchen is warm, refrigerate the pastry until ready to use.

3. Preheat the oven to 350°F. Lightly butter a 1½- to 2-quart shallow baking dish.

4. Combine the peaches and figs in a large bowl; add the lime juice and toss to blend. In a small bowl combine the remaining 2 tablespoons flour, the remaining 2 tablespoons sugar, and the cinnamon; stir to blend. Sprinkle this over the fruit. Fold gently, just to blend without crushing the fruit.

5. Spoon the fruit into the prepared baking dish. Sprinkle the cold pastry crumbs evenly over the fruit.

6. Bake until the top is golden brown and the fruit is bubbly, 35 to 40 minutes. Allow to cool slightly. Sprinkle the crumble with confectioners' sugar and serve warm, with the ice cream.

dried fig and apple oatmeal crisp

makes 8 servings

*S*pruce up the ubiquitous all-apple crisp by adding some dried figs and a
ring of oatmeal and almonds. Serve the crisp warm, with a scoop of
vanilla ice cream on top.

❧

½ cup coarsely chopped natural (unskinned) whole almonds

¾ cup packed light brown sugar

⅓ cup plus 2 tablespoons all-purpose flour

1½ pounds Granny Smith or other tart apples, quartered, peeled, cored,
thinly sliced (about 4 cups)

8 ounces moist dried Calimyrna or Black Mission figs, stems trimmed,
finely chopped (about 1¼ cups)

2 tablespoons diced (¼-inch) crystallized ginger

1 cup old-fashioned or quick-cooking rolled oats (see Note)

1 teaspoon ground ginger

½ teaspoon salt

6 tablespoons unsalted butter, cut into small pieces, at room temperature

Vanilla ice cream, vanilla frozen yogurt, or heavy cream

❧

1. Preheat the oven to 350°F. Lightly butter a shallow 13 × 9-inch baking dish or a deep pie
   plate.
2. Spread the almonds in an ungreased baking pan and bake until lightly toasted, 8 to 10
   minutes. Allow to cool.
3. Combine ¼ cup of the brown sugar and the 2 tablespoons flour in a large bowl. Add the

apples, figs, and crystallized ginger; toss to combine. Spread the mixture in the prepared baking dish.

4. Combine the oats, the remaining ½ cup brown sugar, the remaining ⅓ cup flour, the ground ginger, and the salt in a large bowl; stir to blend. Add the butter and work it into the mixture with a pastry blender, fork, or your fingers until the mixture is crumbly. Sprinkle the oatmeal mixture evenly over the apple mixture.

5. Bake until the crumbs are well browned and the apples are tender, 45 to 55 minutes. Serve lukewarm or at room temperature, with a scoop of vanilla ice cream or frozen yogurt or a drizzle of heavy cream.

note: There are four types of oats available: steel-cut, old-fashioned, quick-cooking, and instant. If you are using the steel-cut or old-fashioned oats, whirl them in a food processor for 30 seconds to break the flakes up a little. The quick-cooking oats can be used straight from the package. Do not use instant oatmeal for this recipe.

fresh fig clafouti

makes 6 to 8 servings

Use a variety of fresh figs for this pudding-like dessert. The mixture of flavors, sizes, and colors is pleasing to the palate and to the eye.

❧

¼ cup plus 2 tablespoons sugar

1½ cups whole milk

1 cup heavy cream

4 large eggs

1 teaspoon pure vanilla extract

1 cup all-purpose flour

¼ teaspoon salt

1 pound fresh figs, mixed sizes and colors, stems trimmed, halved lengthwise or quartered if large

1 tablespoon unsalted butter, cut into small pieces

❧

1. Preheat the oven to 350°F. Generously butter a 10-inch pie plate or other round shallow baking dish. Sprinkle evenly with 1 tablespoon of the sugar.
2. Whisk the milk, cream, eggs, and vanilla together in a large measuring cup or a bowl with a pouring spout until blended. Sift the flour, ¼ cup sugar, and the salt into a separate large bowl. Gradually whisk the milk mixture into the flour mixture until fairly smooth. Pour the batter through a strainer into the prepared pie plate, pressing down on any lumps of flour in the strainer to dissolve them.
3. Arrange the figs, cut side up, on top of the batter. Dot the surface with the pieces of butter.
4. Bake until the edges are puffed and golden and the clafouti is cooked in the center, 50 to 55 minutes. Transfer the dish to a wire rack, and sprinkle the top evenly with the remaining 1 tablespoon sugar while it's still warm. Serve warm or at room temperature, spooned onto serving plates.

flourless dried fig and chocolate cake with fig custard sauce

*T*his cake, called Chocolate and Fig Torte on the menu at Hayes Street Grill in San Francisco, was a must-try. It's a rich, moist cake with an intense chocolate flavor. The figs add a distinctive taste and a pleasant crunch. Patricia Unterman, the owner of Hayes Street Grill, generously offered to have her pastry chef, Karen Smithson, share their recipe with me. A great big thank-you to both of you! At Hayes Street the cake is served with a cool, delicate vanilla custard sauce. As an alternative I offer a fig custard sauce. A few fresh berries—raspberries, blueberries, or sliced strawberries in season—look pretty as a garnish and add a nice contrast. Make the cake the day before you plan to serve it—it needs to chill overnight.

❧

6 ounces moist dried Calimyrna or Black Mission figs (10 to 12 figs), stems trimmed

7 ounces good-quality semisweet chocolate, coarsely chopped

8 tablespoons (1 stick) unsalted butter, cut into pieces

2 tablespoons Cognac

6 large eggs, separated

⅓ cup plus 3 tablespoons sugar

Pinch of salt

Fig Custard Sauce (recipe follows)

2 cups fresh raspberries, blueberries, or hulled and sliced strawberries

❧

1. Preheat the oven to 300°F. Lightly butter the bottom and sides of a 9-inch springform pan and place it in a larger baking pan. Heat a kettle of water.

2. Combine the figs and ⅔ cup water in a small saucepan; heat to a boil. Cover and cook over very low heat until the figs have softened and only about 2 tablespoons liquid remains, about 10 minutes. Allow to cool. If the liquid has evaporated, add 2 tablespoons hot water. Puree the figs and liquid in a food processor. There should be about ⅔ cup fig paste. Set aside.

3. Combine the chocolate and butter in the top of a double boiler set over simmering water. Stir occasionally until melted.

4. Remove the top of the double boiler from the heat; add the fig paste and the Cognac; stir to blend.

5. Beat the egg yolks and the 3 tablespoons sugar in an electric mixer until light and fluffy, about 5 minutes.

6. In a separate bowl, beat the egg whites and salt on medium speed until soft peaks begin to form. Gradually add the remaining ⅓ cup sugar, beating until the whites are stiff and satiny but not dry.

7. Fold the chocolate mixture into the yolks until blended. Then fold the whites, in two additions, into the chocolate mixture until blended.

8. Transfer the batter to the prepared pan, and cover the pan tightly with aluminum foil. Place the baking pan (holding the cake pan) in the oven. Add enough boiling water to come halfway up the sides of the springform pan.

9. Bake for 1½ hours. Lift the foil and take a look at the cake. It should be be firm in the center and pulling away from the sides of the pan. Remove the pan from the oven. Lift the springform pan from the water bath and let it cool on a folded kitchen towel. Refrigerate the cooled cake, tightly covered, overnight before removing it from the springform pan.

10. To remove the cake from the pan, run a spatula around the sides of the pan. Loosen and remove the sides. Run a thin flexible spatula along the bottom of the cake, and slide it onto a flat cake dish.

11. To serve, cut the cake into thin wedges. Place a wedge of cake in the center of each plate, and spoon about 2 tablespoons of the Fig Custard Sauce on the side. Garnish each serving with a few berries.

fig custard sauce

❧

12 ounces dried Calimyrna figs, stems trimmed, coarsely chopped (about 1½ cups)

1¾ cups whole milk, plus more if needed

½ cup heavy cream

4 egg yolks

½ cup sugar

1 teaspoon pure vanilla extract

❧

1. Combine the figs and 1 cup water in a small saucepan and heat to a boil. Cook, covered, over low heat until the figs are very soft and almost all the water has been absorbed, 15 to 20 minutes. Cool slightly. Then place the figs and the milk in a food processor and process until smooth.

2. Set a strainer over a medium bowl and strain the fig mixture, pressing down hard on the figs to extract as much flavor as possible. Discard the solids in the strainer. Add the heavy cream to the fig-flavored milk. There should be 2 cups: add additional milk if needed.

3. Beat the egg yolks and the sugar together in a medium bowl until the sugar has dissolved. Combine the yolk mixture and the fig cream in the top of a double boiler. Cook over simmering water, stirring frequently, until the cream has thickened enough to thickly coat the back of a metal spoon, or a thermometer registers 170° to 180°F, about 20 minutes.

4. Strain the custard sauce into a medium bowl; stir in the vanilla. Refrigerate the sauce until well chilled, about 3 hours. The custard sauce can be made up to 2 days before serving. It will thicken more as it chills.

dried fig cinnamon scones

Preserve fresh fig jam (see recipes, pages 149–154) in the summer and eat it all winter spooned onto these delicate cinnamon and dried fig scones.

❧

2 cups all-purpose flour

⅓ cup sugar

1 tablespoon baking powder

2 teaspoons ground cinnamon

½ teaspoon salt

½ teaspoon grated lemon zest, optional

8 tablespoons (1 stick) cold butter, cut into small pieces

8 ounces dried Calimyrna figs, stems trimmed, finely chopped (about 1¼ cups)

½ cup finely chopped walnuts, optional

½ cup heavy cream, plus more for brushing the scones

1 large egg

Coarse baker's sugar or cinnamon sugar

❧

1. Preheat the oven to 425°F. Place a rack in the center of the oven. Lightly butter a baking sheet.
2. Combine the flour, sugar, baking powder, cinnamon, and salt in the bowl of a food processor. Pulse just to combine. Add the grated lemon zest, if using.
3. Add the butter, a few pieces at a time, through the feed tube, pulsing just until the mixture forms coarse crumbs.
4. Transfer the mixture to a large bowl. Add the figs and walnuts, if using, and toss to coat.

Whisk the ½ cup heavy cream and the egg together in a small bowl. Add this to the flour mixture and gently mix together just until all the ingredients are evenly moistened. Gather the dough together with your hands and form it into a large ball. Turn the dough out onto a lightly floured surface and gently knead it for just a few turns, so that a cohesive ball forms.

5. Pat the dough out to form an 8-inch round, and cut it into 8 wedges. Arrange the wedges on the baking sheet. Lightly brush the tops with a little cream, and sprinkle each with coarse sugar or cinnamon sugar.

6. Bake until the tops are golden brown, 12 to 15 minutes. Cool on a wire rack.

dried fig and banana walnut muffins

*M*oist and tender, these banana and fig muffins freeze well. I make a batch whenever our bananas are ripening faster than we can eat them.

❧

1½ cups all-purpose flour

2 teaspoons baking powder

1 teaspoon baking soda, sieved

½ teaspoon ground cinnamon

½ teaspoon salt

6 ounces dried Calimyrna or Black Mission figs, stems trimmed, cut into ¼-inch pieces (about 1 cup)

½ cup coarsely chopped walnuts, plus ½ cup broken walnuts

1½ cups mashed ripe banana (3 or 4 bananas)

⅔ cup packed light brown sugar

⅓ cup unsalted butter, melted

1 large egg

1 teaspoon pure vanilla extract

❧

1. Preheat the oven to 350°F. Lightly butter 20 muffin cups, or coat them with nonstick cooking spray. Add 2 tablespoons water each to any empty muffin cups.
2. Combine the flour, baking powder, baking soda, cinnamon, and salt in a large bowl. Add the figs and the chopped walnuts; toss to coat.

3. In a separate bowl whisk the banana, brown sugar, melted butter, egg, and vanilla together until blended. Add this to the dry ingredients all at once, and fold until evenly moistened.

4. Divide the batter among the muffin cups. Sprinkle the tops evenly with the broken walnuts. Bake until the tops are golden and a toothpick inserted in the center comes out clean, 20 to 22 minutes.

5. Cool on a wire rack before removing the muffins from the pans.

fig heaven

dried fig and chocolate biscotti

makes about 2 dozen biscotti

*D*ried figs, while not traditionally found in biscotti, go well with the walnuts and chopped chocolate in this version. These biscotti are less dry than most because of the moisture contributed by the figs.

❧

8 tablespoons (1 stick) unsalted butter, at room temperature

¾ cup sugar

2 large eggs

2¼ cups all-purpose flour

1½ teaspoons baking powder

½ teaspoon salt

6 ounces dried Calimyrna figs, stems trimmed, diced small (about 1 cup packed)

1 cup coarsely chopped walnuts

6 ounces good-quality bittersweet chocolate, chopped (about ¾ cup)

❧

1. Preheat the oven to 350°F. Line a large baking sheet with parchment paper.
2. Beat the butter and sugar in the large bowl of an electric mixer until light. Beat in the eggs, one at a time, until blended. In another bowl, stir 2 cups of the flour, the baking powder, and the salt together until blended. Gradually beat the flour mixture into the butter mixture until incorporated.
3. Combine the figs, walnuts, chocolate, and the remaining ¼ cup flour in a medium bowl; stir to coat. Stir into the dough.
4. Turn the dough out onto a lightly floured surface and divide it in half. With floured hands, shape each portion of dough into a log about 12 inches long and 2½ inches wide. Using a

long, wide, flat spatula, slide the logs onto the parchment-lined cookie sheet, positioning them about 4 inches apart. (The logs will spread considerably when baked.)

5. Bake until light golden brown, about 30 minutes. Slide the parchment onto a wire rack and let the logs cool for 20 minutes. Reduce the oven temperature to 300°F.

6. Carefully slide the logs onto a cutting board. Using a sharp knife, slice each log diagonally into ¾-inch-wide biscotti, making one firm cut for each slice. Transfer the slices, cut sides down, to the baking sheet. Bake until dry to the touch and pale gold, about 20 minutes. Cool on a wire rack.

nana's fig-stuffed cookies

makes about 3 dozen cookies

*M*ade with a cream cheese pastry, these delicate cookies played a promi-
nent part in my career choice. My grandmother Nana, as we called
her, was well known for her delicious baking. I spent many Saturday afternoons during my childhood helping her keep the canning pot in her sewing
room filled with her famous cookies. These are only one of the many cookies
Nana taught me to make. They keep well for only about 5 days at room temperature, but they freeze well, as does the dough.

❧

4 ounces cream cheese, cut into small pieces, at room temperature

8 tablespoons (1 stick) unsalted butter, cut into small pieces, at room temperature

1 cup unbleached all-purpose flour

2 tablespoons sugar

½ teaspoon salt

¾ cup packed, coarsely chopped dried Calimyrna or Black Mission figs (about 10 figs)

⅓ cup fresh orange juice or water

¼ teaspoon grated orange zest

2 tablespoons finely chopped walnuts

1 egg yolk beaten with 1 tablespoon milk

Confectioners' sugar

❧

1. Place the cream cheese, butter, flour, sugar, and salt in the bowl of a food processor, and
   process just until a dough begins to form. Turn the dough out onto a floured surface and

gather it into a ball. Place it on a piece of aluminum foil, flatten it slightly, wrap it tightly, and refrigerate it until well chilled, at least 2 hours.

2. Combine the figs and orange juice in a small saucepan. Cover and cook over low heat, stirring occasionally, until the liquid has been absorbed, about 15 minutes. Cool slightly. Place the figs in a food processor and process until the consistency is fairly smooth. The puree should be very stiff, almost a paste. Transfer it to a bowl and stir in the orange zest and walnuts. Set this filling aside until ready to use. It can be made a day ahead.

3. Preheat the oven to 350°F. Lightly butter two cookie sheets.

4. Divide the dough in half, and roll one half out on lightly floured board or pastry cloth, using a rolling pin covered with a floured stocking to $\frac{1}{8}$-inch thickness. Cut $2\frac{1}{2}$-inch rounds. Drop a rounded teaspoonful of the fig mixture in the center of each round, and fold the cookies in half to make half-circles. Pinch the edges together. Stack the scraps and re-roll. Repeat with the remaining dough and filling.

5. Transfer the cookies to the prepared cookie sheets. Lightly brush the top of each cookie with the beaten egg mixture. Bake until golden brown, about 20 minutes. Let cool on a wire rack. Dust with confectioners' sugar while still warm.

chunky chocolate, dried fig, and pecan cookies

makes about 3 dozen cookies

*P*ut a platter of these cookies out and watch them disappear. Nuggets of semisweet chocolate, dried figs, and meaty pecans are held together by an intensely chocolate batter. For another flavor dimension add 2 teaspoons instant espresso coffee powder to the egg mixture in step 4.

❧

8 tablespoons (1 stick) unsalted butter, cut into 1-inch pieces

3 ounces unsweetened chocolate, coarsely chopped

1¼ cups all-purpose flour

¾ teaspoon baking powder

½ teaspoon salt

2 large eggs

¾ cup packed light brown sugar

½ cup granulated sugar

1 teaspoon pure vanilla extract

6 ounces moist dried Calimyrna or Black Mission figs, cut into ¼-inch dice (about 1 cup)

1 cup coarsely chopped semisweet chocolate or chocolate chips

1 cup coarsely chopped pecans

❧

1. Preheat the oven to 350°F. Lightly butter two cookie sheets, or line them with parchment paper.
2. Combine the butter and chocolate in a small saucepan and melt over very low heat (or combine in a glass bowl and melt in a microwave oven for about 1 minute). Stir to blend. Set aside until cooled, about 15 minutes.
3. Sift the flour, baking powder, and salt onto a sheet of waxed paper. Set it aside.
4. Combine the eggs, brown sugar, granulated sugar, and vanilla in the bowl of an electric mixer. Beat until light and fluffy.
5. Slowly beat in the cooled chocolate mixture until blended. Gradually add the flour mixture, beating slowly just until blended. The batter will be very stiff. Stir the figs, chopped chocolate, and pecans into the batter by hand.
6. Using a generously rounded tablespoon, drop the batter onto the prepared baking sheets, leaving at least 2 inches between cookies. Bake until the cookies are set on top, 10 to 15 minutes, turning the pan halfway through the baking time. Cool the cookies on the cookie sheets on a wire rack before removing them.

dried fig, walnut, and chunky chip sugar cookies

makes 4 dozen cookies

A brown sugar and vanilla batter makes these a figgy version of the classic chocolate chip cookie. This is a totally addictive cookie.

❧

8 ounces (2 sticks) unsalted butter, at room temperature

1¾ cups packed light brown sugar

3 large eggs

1 teaspoon pure vanilla extract

2¾ cups all-purpose flour

1 teaspoon baking soda

1 teaspoon ground cinnamon

½ teaspoon salt

Two 8-ounce packages dried Calimyrna figs, stems trimmed,
cut into ¼-inch pieces (about 2½ cups)

2 cups coarsely chopped walnuts

2 cups coarsely chopped semisweet chocolate or chocolate chips

❧

1. Preheat the oven to 350°F. Lightly butter two large baking sheets, or line them with parchment paper.
2. Cream the butter in the large bowl of an electric mixer. Add the sugar and beat until light
   and fluffy, scraping down the sides of the bowl with a rubber spatula as needed.
3. Beat in the eggs, one at a time, beating well after each addition. Add the vanilla; beat until
   blended.

4. Sift the flour, baking soda, cinnamon, and salt together in another bowl. Gradually beat the flour mixture into the butter mixture on the lowest speed, just until combined. Finish combining with a rubber spatula.

5. Add the figs, walnuts, and chocolate and stir just until blended.

6. Using a heaping tablespoon, drop the batter onto the prepared baking sheets, placing the cookies at least 2 inches apart.

7. Bake until the edges of the cookies are golden and the tops are set, 13 to 15 minutes. Cool slightly on the cookie sheet before removing to a wire rack to cool.

homemade fig newtons

*F*or many of us, Fig Newtons are the cookie of our childhood memories. My husband was convinced they were named for his hometown, Newton, New Jersey, but the Nabisco Web site claims they were named for either Sir Issac Newton or Newton, Massachusetts. In any case, they are one of the most popular cookies in the United States. This rendition is a superlative version of the store-bought Fig Newton.

❧

1 pound dried Calimyrna or Black Mission figs, stems trimmed, halved
(about 2½ cups)

2 teaspoons pure vanilla extract

12 tablespoons (1½ sticks) unsalted butter, at room temperature

1 cup sugar

3 cups all-purpose flour

1½ teaspoons baking powder

½ teaspoon ground cinnamon

½ teaspoon salt

2 large eggs

1 egg yolk beaten with 2 tablespoons milk

❧

1. Combine the figs and 2 cups water in a medium saucepan, and heat to a boil. Reduce the heat and simmer, covered, until almost all the water has been absorbed and the figs are very soft, 30 to 35 minutes. Cool slightly. (Excess moisture will be absorbed as the figs cool.) Puree the figs in a food processor. Add the vanilla to the puree and set it aside.

2. Combine the butter and sugar in the large bowl of an electric mixer, and beat until light and fluffy.

3. Sift the flour, baking powder, cinnamon, and salt together in another bowl.

4. Add the eggs, one at a time, to the butter mixture, beating well after each addition. Gradually beat in the flour mixture just until blended.

5. With floured hands, gather the dough into a ball and flatten it into a disc. Wrap it in aluminum foil and refrigerate until chilled, about 2 hours. (The dough can be chilled overnight; let it stand at room temperature for about 30 minutes to soften slightly before attempting to roll it out.)

6. Preheat the oven to 350°F. Cut two pieces of parchment paper to fit your cookie sheets.

7. Divide the dough into four equal portions. Refrigerate the unrolled portions until you are ready to roll them out.

8. Gently roll one portion of the dough out on a lightly floured pastry cloth, using a rolling pin covered with a floured stocking, to form a strip about 15 inches long and 5 inches wide. Spread ½ cup of the fig puree down the center of the dough in a strip approximately 1½ inches wide. Fold the long sides of the dough toward the center, slightly overlapping to enclose the filling. Using two long flat spatulas, slide the dough, seam side down, onto one of the pieces of parchment. (If your spatula isn't long enough, the strips can be cut in half to make it easier to transfer them to the parchment.)

9. Repeat with the remaining dough and filling, placing two long strips of filled dough lengthwise, or four halved strips of dough crosswise, about 3 inches apart on each sheet of parchment. Slide the parchment onto the cookie sheets. Lightly brush the egg and milk mixture over the surface of the dough.

10. Bake until the edges are browned, 25 to 30 minutes, changing the positions of the baking sheets halfway through baking. Cool on the cookie sheets on a wire rack. Then, using a thin sharp knife, cut each strip crosswise at 1½- to 2-inch intervals.

poached dried figs in phyllo flowers with spiced syrup

makes 12 servings

*T*hink of these as treasure-filled purses of feathery phyllo, or as golden flowers sprinkled with green pistachios. Serve them in a pool of spiced syrup or shower them with a dusting of confectioners' sugar. Either way, they are sublime.

❧

¾ cup sugar

One 3-inch cinnamon stick

1 star anise pod

1 whole clove

1 cardamom pod

1 bay leaf

1 strip lemon zest, ½ × 2 inches

12 large dried Calimyrna figs, stems left intact

¼ cup coarsely chopped unsalted skinned pistachios, plus ½ cup finely chopped

6 tablespoons (¾ stick) unsalted butter

One 16-ounce package frozen phyllo dough, thawed in the refrigerator

Confectioners' sugar, optional

❧

1. Combine 3 cups water and the sugar in a medium saucepan; heat to a boil, stirring, to dissolve the sugar. Add the cinnamon, star anise, clove, cardamom, bay leaf, and lemon zest.

Cook, covered, over medium heat for 5 minutes. Add the figs and cook, covered, over medium-low heat until they are plumped, about 45 minutes. Transfer the figs and the syrup (there should be about 1½ cups) to a bowl and refrigerate until very cold. This can be prepared 1 or more days ahead.

2. Drain the cold poached figs, reserving the syrup. Heat the syrup in a medium saucepan to a boil, and boil, uncovered, over medium heat until reduced to about 1 cup. Refrigerate until chilled. (See Step 8: If you prefer to garnish with confectioners' sugar, skip this reduction and reserve the syrup for another use.)

3. Blot the figs dry on a folded kitchen towel. Using a small paring knife, cut a half-circle flap in the bottom of each fig. With your fingertip, press the soft interior of the fig to make a space for the pistachios. Stuff about 1 teaspoon of the coarsely chopped pistachios into each fig; replace the flap.

4. Preheat the oven to 350°F. Lightly butter a 12-cup muffin pan.

5. Melt the butter in a small saucepan over low heat or in the microwave. Let it stand until the white solids have settled. Pour off and reserve the clear (clarified) butter. Discard the solids.

6. Unwrap the phyllo and remove 8 sheets. Using a ruler, cut the stack of phyllo sheets into six 5-inch squares. Rewrap the remainder and reserve it for other use. Keep the cut phyllo covered with a dampened kitchen towel so it won't dry out. Working with four 5-inch squares at a time, brush each one with clarified butter and then restack them, alternating the corners of the squares to create a flower-like pattern. Place one of the pistachio-stuffed figs upright in the center, loosely gather up the edges, and gently pinch the phyllo around the stem of the fig to resemble a drawstring purse. Place the "purse" in a muffin cup. Gently separate the phyllo corners to make "flower petals," allowing the stem of the dried fig to be visible. Brush the edges of the phyllo with a little butter so they will turn golden as they bake. Sprinkle the phyllo petals with about ½ teaspoon of the finely chopped pistachios. Repeat with the remaining phyllo and figs to make 12 "flowers."

7. Bake until the phyllo is golden, 12 to 15 minutes. Cool slightly in the muffin tins and then use a thin spatula to carefully transfer them to a wire rack to cool.

8. Serve each flower on a shallow pool of the reserved chilled spiced syrup. Or for a less formal dessert, omit the syrup and simply sprinkle the "flowers" with confectioners' sugar.

fresh figs with mascarpone and orange caramel sauce

makes 4 servings

*W*hen a friend described this dessert to me after eating it at a restaurant, I just had to give it a try. My thanks to the chef, wherever you are, for coming up with this unique combination.

❧

½ cup sugar

1 cup heavy cream, at room temperature

1½ teaspoons grated orange zest

½ teaspoon pure vanilla extract

8 large ripe figs, any variety, stems trimmed, halved lengthwise

2 large seedless oranges, peel and pith removed, sectioned

½ cup (approximately) mascarpone

❧

1. Sprinkle the sugar evenly in a heavy 9-inch skillet. Cook, without stirring, over medium-high heat, swirling the pan from time to time, until the sugar has dissolved and turned a dark golden brown. Add the heavy cream all at once; it will sputter and begin to boil rapidly. Cook over medium heat, stirring gently, until the hardened sugar dissolves in the hot cream and the cream begins to thicken, about 5 minutes. Stir in the orange zest. Pour the sauce into a measuring cup and allow it to cool slightly. Add the vanilla. Serve the sauce warm or at room temperature. (The sauce can be made ahead and reheated to soften.)

2. Arrange 4 fig halves in a circle, cut side up, on each of four large dessert plates. Place 4 orange sections between the figs. Place a rounded teaspoon of mascarpone on the center of each fig half. Drizzle about ¼ cup of the caramel sauce in ribbons over each serving of figs and oranges. Serve at once.

fresh figs and peaches in wine

makes 4 servings

A *refreshing dessert for a hot summer's night because there's no cooking required. Use either red or white wine and the juiciest, sweetest fruit you can find.*

❧

4 to 6 large ripe figs, any variety, stems trimmed, halved or quartered

2 or 3 large ripe freestone peaches, peeled, cut into thick wedges

2 teaspoons sugar

2 cups slightly chilled white or red wine

❧

Distribute the figs and peach wedges among four dessert bowls or large stemmed glasses. Sprinkle each portion of fruit with ½ teaspoon of the sugar. Splash each with about ½ cup of the wine, and serve at once.

fresh figs and summer fruits in honey wine syrup with lemon thyme

makes 6 to 8 servings

*C*ombine the best fruits of the season in this light, honey-sweetened syrup, which can be made ahead, and serve well chilled. Add whatever herbs you can find to the syrup. I like the savory nature of thyme, but mint, basil, lavender, even lemon balm, will all be lovely. Make sure to cut the fruit in uniformly sized pieces so they can be enjoyed easily with a dessert spoon.

2 cups dry white wine

¼ cup sugar

3 tablespoons full-flavored honey

1 tablespoon small fresh lemon thyme sprigs, optional

4 or more firm ripe green or black figs (or a few different varieties), stems trimmed, quartered or cubed, depending on size

4 cups fresh fruit (pitted cherries, ripe cantaloupe, blueberries, raspberries, strawberries, peaches, nectarines, apricots, plums, or whatever is ripe in the market), cut up as necessary

1 tablespoon thyme blossoms, if available, or substitute 1 tablespoon thyme leaves

1. Combine the wine and 1 cup water in a small saucepan; heat to a boil. Boil gently for 5 minutes. Then stir in the sugar and honey; cook, stirring, until the sugar has dissolved. Stir in the thyme, if using, cover, and let steep for 20 minutes.

2. Combine the figs and fruits in a heat-resistant bowl. Strain the warm syrup and pour it over the fruit. Refrigerate, covered, until well chilled, at least 4 hours.

3. To serve, use a slotted spoon to divide the fruit among six to eight dessert bowls. Ladle the syrup over the fruit. Garnish each with a thyme blossom, if available, and serve.

fresh fruit in honey-vanilla wine syrup: Instead of the lemon thyme or other herbs, flavor the syrup with vanilla: Cook the syrup as described in Step 1. When the sugar has dissolved, allow the syrup to cool to lukewarm; then stir in 2 teaspoons pure vanilla extract, and proceed with Step 2. Omit the thyme blossoms and garnish with thyme leaves.

warm fresh fig fritters

*B*atter-dipped fresh figs are fried until the coating is golden and cake-like. Serve them warm with a dusting of confectioners' sugar or a drizzle of vanilla honey syrup.

❧

½ cup milk

1 large egg

¾ cup all-purpose flour

½ teaspoon baking powder

Pinch of salt

2 cups (approximately) vegetable oil for frying

12 large or 16 small ripe figs, any variety, stems trimmed

Confectioners' sugar or Honey Vanilla Syrup (recipe follows)

❧

1. Whisk the milk and egg together in a medium bowl. Stir in the flour, baking powder, and salt until the mixture is smooth.

2. Heat the oil in a heavy deep skillet or saucepan over medium heat until it is hot enough to sizzle and brown a crust of bread, about 365°F on a thermometer. Using tongs, dip the figs, one at a time, into the batter, turning to thickly coat. Fry 1 or 2 fritters at a time in the hot oil until golden all over, about 2 minutes per side.

3. Drain the fritters briefly on a double layer of paper towels, then transfer them to a wire rack and sprinkle them generously with confectioners' sugar. Or place them on individual dessert plates and drizzle with Honey Vanilla Syrup. Serve while they are still warm.

honey vanilla syrup

❧

¼ cup sugar

½ cup honey

1 vanilla bean, split lengthwise

❧

1. Combine 2 cups water and the sugar in a medium saucepan and heat to a boil, stirring until the sugar has dissolved. Stir in the honey until blended. Using the tip of a teaspoon, scrape the seeds from the vanilla bean and add the seeds to the syrup; add the bean also.
2. Boil gently, uncovered, over medium heat until the syrup is slightly thickened and reduced to about 1½ cups. Remove the vanilla bean. Chill the syrup until cold, about 3 hours.

chocolate-stuffed fresh figs with vanilla custard sauce

*M*ake the custard sauce a day or two ahead so it has time to become infused with the flavor of the vanilla bean. Prepare the figs just before serving—the prep time is a matter of minutes and the baking time is less than 15 minutes. A few blueberries, raspberries, or sliced strawberries strewn over the chilled custard sauce make a bright garnish.

❧

2 cups whole milk

⅓ cup plus 3 teaspoons sugar

1 vanilla bean, split lengthwise

4 large egg yolks

6 large firm ripe figs, any variety, stems trimmed

2 tablespoons (approximately) unsalted butter, melted

6 pieces (about ½-inch square) good-quality semisweet chocolate

Blueberries, raspberries, or sliced strawberries, optional

❧

1. Combine the milk and ⅓ cup sugar in the top of a double boiler; add the vanilla bean. Place the pan directly over medium heat and stir to dissolve the sugar. When the milk is hot, remove the pan from the heat and let it stand, covered, for about 30 minutes. Remove the vanilla bean and reserve it.

2. Whisk the egg yolks in a medium bowl until blended. Stir about half of the warm milk into the yolks until blended. Add the egg yolk mixture to the remaining warm milk.

3. Pour an inch of water into the bottom of the double boiler and heat to a simmer; place the top of the double boiler over the bottom. Cook the custard, stirring gently but thoroughly with a metal spoon, until the sauce is thick enough to coat the back of the spoon, 170° to 180°F on a thermometer.

4. Pour the sauce through a strainer into a small bowl. Using the tip of a spoon, scrape the seeds from the reserved vanilla bean into the strained sauce; stir. Place the bean in the sauce for added flavor. Refrigerate, uncovered, until well chilled. Then cover and keep chilled until ready to serve. Remove the vanilla bean before serving.

5. About 30 minutes before serving, preheat the oven to 400°F. Coat a shallow baking dish, just large enough to hold the figs without crowding, with a little butter.

6. Cut an X about ½-inch deep in the top of each fig. Push a chunk of chocolate down into the center of each fig. Place the figs in the prepared baking dish. Brush each fig lightly with melted butter and sprinkle ½ teaspoon sugar over each one. Bake until the chocolate has melted, 12 to 15 minutes.

7. Ladle about ⅓ cup of the vanilla custard sauce into each of six shallow bowls or dessert plates. Set a hot fig in the center of each. Garnish the custard with a few berries, if using, and serve.

fig heaven

dried fig, orange, and chocolate bonbons

makes 20 to 24 pieces

*D*ried figs and chocolate are a heavenly combination. These little spheres of ground fig, chocolate, walnuts, and candied orange zest are dipped in melted chocolate. Use the best chocolate you can find for this recipe. These are pretty served in pleated foil candy cups.

❧

6 ounces moist dried Calimyrna or Black Mission figs, stems trimmed, cut up (about 1 cup packed)

½ cup broken walnuts

½ cup bittersweet chocolate chips or slab chocolate, chopped

4 ounces candied orange peel, cut into ½-inch pieces (about ½ cup)

4 ounces bittersweet slab chocolate, coarsely chopped

3 tablespoons unsalted butter

❧

1. Coarsely chop the figs in a food processor. Add the walnuts, chocolate chips, and the orange peel. Process until the mixture is chopped together and gummy enough to form a ball.

2. Keeping hands wet with water, squeeze the mixture, 1 tablespoon at a time, into firm round balls. Place the balls on a parchment paper–lined tray or a cookie sheet. When the balls are formed, refrigerate until very cold, about 1 hour or more.

3. Combine the coarsely chopped chocolate and butter in a small saucepan and melt, stirring often, over low heat until smooth. Using tongs, dip each ball into the chocolate to coat

about half of it; let the excess drip off. Place the chocolate-dipped fig balls on a wire rack set on a cookie sheet until the chocolate is set. (To set the chocolate quickly, refrigerate the balls.) When the chocolate is set, place the bonbons in pleated candy papers and store in the refrigerator until ready to serve. These keep for 2 weeks or more.

STICKY BUSINESS

Make easy work of chopping dried figs by using the food processor, but to prevent sticking, first brush or spray the bowl and metal blade lightly with a thin film of flavorless vegetable oil. The same vegetable oil–coating trick works on a knife blade or scissors when cutting or snipping figs by hand.

dried figs and apricots
in vanilla wine syrup

makes 4 to 6 servings

This is a simple dessert to make ahead. Keep it on hand for a quick fix of something sweet after dinner.

❦

1 bottle (750 ml) Gewürztraminer or Johannisberg Riesling wine

⅔ cup sugar

1 vanilla bean, split lengthwise

8 ounces dried Calimyrna figs (12 to 14 figs)

Two 3-inch cinnamon sticks, broken in half

4 ounces (about 1 cup packed) dried apricots (about 12 halves)

½ cup crème fraîche, fromage blanc, or yogurt, optional

1 tablespoon toasted sliced natural (unskinned) almonds, optional

❦

1. Combine the wine and sugar in a large saucepan. Heat to a boil over medium heat, stirring, until the sugar has dissolved. Scrape the seeds from the vanilla bean; add the seeds and the bean to the syrup. Add the figs and cinnamon sticks. Cook, covered, over medium-low heat for 20 minutes: add the apricots and cook until the fruits are plumped and tender, about 25 minutes more.

2. Using a slotted spoon, transfer the fruit, cinnamon sticks, and vanilla bean to a heat-resistant bowl. Boil the wine syrup, uncovered, until it is reduced to about 2 cups. Pour the syrup over the figs and stir to blend.

3. Refrigerate until well chilled, about 4 hours. Eat plain or with a spoonful of crème fraîche, yogurt, or fromage blanc on top. Garnish with almonds if desired.

baked apples stuffed with dried figs and walnuts

The ordinary baked apple is glorified in this recipe with a stuffing of dried figs and walnuts. Serve these plain, sitting in a pool of heavy cream, or, for a special occasion, with my Vanilla Custard Sauce. Time the baking so they can be served warm.

❦

6 large baking apples (Rome Beauties, Pippins, or Golden Delicious)

1 teaspoon flavorless vegetable oil

½ cup cut-up (½-inch pieces) dried Calimyrna or Black Mission figs

½ cup coarsely chopped walnuts

4 tablespoons (½ stick) cold unsalted butter, cut into ½-inch pieces

¼ cup packed light brown sugar

½ teaspoon ground cinnamon

1 cup chilled heavy cream or Vanilla Custard Sauce (pages 135–136, Steps 1–4), optional

❦

1. Preheat the oven to 350°F. Lightly butter a 13 × 9-inch baking dish, 10-inch pie plate, or other dish just large enough to hold the apples upright.
2. Core the apples. Using a vegetable peeler, remove a 1-inch-wide strip around the top of each apple. Place the apples in the prepared baking dish.
3. Lightly brush a food processor bowl and blade with the vegetable oil, and finely chop the figs and walnuts. Add the butter, brown sugar, and cinnamon, and process until blended. Transfer the mixture to a small bowl.

4. Stuff the cored apples tightly with the fig mixture, mounding any extra on top of the apples.
5. Bake the apples, basting them occasionally with any juices that form, until tender when pierced with a metal or wooden skewer, 45 minutes to 1 hour. Serve warm, either plain or with heavy cream or Vanilla Custard Sauce.

cinnamon ice cream
with dried fig ripple

*G*etting the dried fig puree to swirl and ripple through homemade ice cream is a bit tricky. The technique that seems to work best is not to stir, but instead to cut the puree in with a couple of swift swipes with two table knives.

❧

6 ounces dried Calimyrna figs, stems trimmed, quartered (about 1 cup packed)

1 cup sugar

2½ cups whole milk

1½ cups heavy cream

Two 3-inch cinnamon sticks

1 teaspoon ground cinnamon

3 large egg yolks

2 teaspoons pure vanilla extract

❧

1. Combine the figs, ⅓ cup of the sugar, and 1½ cups water in a medium saucepan and heat to a boil. Cook, covered, over medium-low heat until almost all the water has been absorbed, about 30 minutes. Allow to cool. Then puree in a food processor; refrigerate until ready to use.

2. Combine the milk, heavy cream, remaining ⅔ cup sugar, cinnamon sticks, and ground cinnamon in a medium saucepan. Heat to a simmer, stirring until the sugar has dissolved, about 5 minutes. Remove from the heat and let stand, covered, for 30 minutes.

3. Beat the egg yolks with a whisk in a large bowl until pale yellow, about 2 minutes. Remove the cinnamon sticks from the milk mixture. Slowly add the warm milk to the egg yolks, stirring gently with the whisk until blended. Return the mixture to the saucepan. Cook, stirring constantly with a large spoon, over low heat until the custard has thickened and lightly coats the back of a spoon; a thermometer should register 170° to 180°F. (To prevent curdling, you can cook the custard in the top of a double boiler set over 1 inch of simmering water.) Strain the mixture into a clean bowl. Refrigerate until very cold. Stir in the vanilla extract.
4. Freeze the custard in an ice cream maker according to the manufacturer's instructions. Transfer it to a large bowl. Working quickly, dot the surface of the ice cream with tablespoons of the fig puree. Using two table knives, quickly cut the fig puree into the ice cream with four or five quick cuts down through the ice cream. Immediately spoon the ice cream into a large freezer container and freeze for several hours, or overnight, before serving.

ICE CREAM MAKERS

There are many different types of ice cream and sorbet makers on the market. I have been using my simple Oster Ice Cream Maker for years. It has a metal canister that sits in a layered solution of ice and salt and turns out lovely smooth sorbets and ice creams every time.

fresh fig and lime sorbet

makes about 1 quart

*F*ig sorbet captures the very essence of fresh figs and is best enjoyed when the fruit is at its ripest. The simple syrup base is flavored with fresh limes, the one citrus that is bountiful and inexpensive during the summer. Make the sugar syrup for the sorbet several hours ahead, or a day in advance, so that it will have plenty of time to chill.

❧

¾ cup sugar

1½ pounds ripe figs, any variety, stems trimmed, peeled if desired (see Note) and cut up (about 3 cups)

½ cup fresh lime juice, or more to taste

❧

1. Combine 2 cups water and the sugar in a medium saucepan. Cook, stirring, until the syrup boils and the sugar has dissolved. Refrigerate until thoroughly chilled.
2. Place the figs in the bowl of a food processor, and puree. Add the puree to the chilled syrup; stir in the lime juice. Taste, and add more lime juice if desired.
3. Prepare the sorbet in an ice cream maker according to the manufacturer's instructions until the mixture begins to freeze. Then scoop it into a storage container, seal tightly, and freeze for several hours or overnight.

note: Test the fig to see if the skin pulls off easily when loosened with the tip of a small paring knife. If it does, peel or partially peel the figs. Black Mission and other purple-skinned figs give the sorbet a rich ruby color, speckled with black if the figs are unpeeled. Green figs will result in a pale pink sorbet, speckled with green if left unpeeled.

quick and easy fresh fig and strawberry sorbet

*E*arly figs and juicy sweet local strawberries appear in my farmers' market simultaneously, so I often pair them in fruit salads, sauces, and in this sorbet. The figs add a smooth sweetness and texture to the sorbet, and the strawberries add their distinctive taste and refreshing tang. Best of all, it doesn't require either simple syrup or an ice cream maker!

❧

1 pound ripe figs, any variety, peeled if desired (see page 10),
cut up (about 2 cups)

1 pint strawberries, stemmed, cut up

½ cup sugar

½ cup crisp fruity white wine, such as Pinot Gris or Riesling, or a rosé

❧

1. Combine the figs, strawberries, sugar, wine, and ½ cup water in the bowl of a food processor. Process until pureed.

2. Transfer the puree to a shallow 13 × 9-inch baking dish and freeze, stirring every hour, until the mixture is firm, 3 to 4 hours.

3. Break the frozen mixture into chunks and place them in the bowl of the food processor. Process, stopping the machine frequently to stir the mixture, until smooth.

4. Transfer the sorbet to a plastic storage container, seal tightly, and freeze until ready to serve.

fresh fig and caramel sauce for ice cream

makes 4 servings

*H*ere are two recipes in one. The first step yields figs caramelized in butter and sugar to spoon over ice cream; the second rewards you with a caramel sauce to combine with the caramelized figs. If you make this ahead of time, you'll need to reheat the caramel sauce. Serve this—figs alone or with the caramel sauce—over vanilla, dulce de leche (caramel), or chocolate ice cream.

❧

fig sauce
2 tablespoons unsalted butter, cut into pieces

6 to 8 ripe figs, any variety, stems trimmed, halved lengthwise

¼ cup sugar

caramel sauce
1 cup heavy cream

1 teaspoon pure vanilla extract

❧

1. Melt the butter in a 9- or 10-inch skillet until foamy. Add the figs, cut side down, and sprinkle evenly with the sugar. Cook, without stirring, over medium heat until the sugar caramelizes and the figs are browned on the bottom, about 5 minutes. Carefully turn the figs over and cook 2 minutes more. Remove the figs to a serving bowl.
2. Add the cream to the skillet and boil, stirring, until it has reduced slightly and the sugar has melted into the cream to make a caramel-colored sauce. Let it stand off the heat for a few minutes. Then stir in the vanilla and add to the figs. Serve warm over ice cream.

dried fig sauce with amaretto

makes 4 to 6 servings

*M*ake this quick-and-easy sauce when you need a topping for ice cream. It is great with chocolate, vanilla, maple pecan or walnut, caramel, or any number of different flavors of ice cream. It is also nice ladled over a poached pear.

❧

8 ounces dried Calimyrna figs, stems trimmed, cut into ¼-inch pieces
(about 1¼ cups)

½ cup sugar

¼ cup amaretto liqueur, bourbon, or Scotch Whiskey

½ teaspoon pure vanilla extract

❧

1. Combine the figs, 2 cups water, and the sugar in a medium saucepan and heat to a boil. Cover, and cook over low heat until the figs are very soft and all but about ½ cup of the water has been absorbed, 15 to 20 minutes. Add the liqueur, bourbon, or whiskey and simmer, uncovered, 5 minutes. Remove from the heat and allow to cool
2. Stir in the vanilla.
3. Refrigerate until chilled. Serve over ice cream or poached fruit.

sweets   147

preserving
fresh figs

I f you have a fig tree in the backyard and it's a good year, chances are you have more figs than you can consume. Figs make fabulous jam and are delicious in a sweet pickle brine. The next best way to preserve a bounteous crop of figs is to freeze them. The following recipes include some expert advice gleaned from Jean Anderson, the author of *Jean Anderson's Green Thumb Preserving Guide.*

sweet pickled fresh figs

✌

2½ pounds small firm ripe Black Mission, green Kadota, or other variety of figs

2 cups cider vinegar

2½ cups sugar

8 whole cloves

8 whole allspice berries

Two 3-inch cinnamon sticks, broken in half

4 strips lemon or orange zest, each ½ × 2 inches

✌

1. Heat a kettle of water.
2. Rinse the figs thoroughly and blot them dry on clean kitchen towels. Do not trim. Prick each one with a skewer (this prevents bursting during processing). Place the figs in a large bowl and cover with boiling water. Let stand until the water cools to room temperature, about 30 minutes.
3. Combine the vinegar, 2 cups water, and the sugar in a large saucepan; heat to a boil, stirring to dissolve the sugar. Drain the figs and carefully lower them into the simmering syrup. Simmer, uncovered, over very low heat for 20 minutes.
4. Meanwhile, boil your canning jars and tops in a large kettle. Invert the sterilized jars on a clean kitchen towel.
5. Turn the canning jars upright, and using tongs or a slotted spoon, carefully arrange the figs in the jars. Place 2 cloves, 2 allspice berries, a piece of cinnamon stick, and a piece of lemon zest in each jar. Ladle the boiling syrup into the jars. Carefully run a small spatula between the fruit and the jar to allow any air bubbles to escape. Fill the jars to within ¼ inch of the rim. Wipe the rims with a clean damp towel and seal.
6. Process in a boiling water bath for 15 minutes. Lift the jars from the bath and let them cool in a dark place. Let the figs stand for at least 1 month so the flavors can develop.

freezing fresh figs

Use only freshly harvested, bruise- and blemish-free, firm ripe figs for freezing. The ascorbic acid (available where canning products are sold) prevents darkening.

❧

3 cups sugar

¾ teaspoon powdered ascorbic acid, optional

4 to 5 pounds fresh firm ripe figs

❧

1. Combine 4 cups water and the sugar in a large saucepan. Heat to a boil, stirring to dissolve the sugar. Stir in the ascorbic acid, if using. Refrigerate until very cold.
2. Rinse the figs with cool water and blot them dry on clean kitchen towels. Trim the stems. Arrange them comfortably (do not squeeze or force them) in pint- or quart-sized freezer containers. (Eight to 10 small figs will fill a pint container, but for larger figs you will need a quart container.) Fill with enough cold syrup to cover the figs (about ¾ cup for pints and 1½ cups for quarts).
3. If the fruit bobs to the top of the container, crinkle a square of aluminum foil and press the fruit down into the syrup. Press the lid on top of the foil, and freeze. These are best used within 3 to 6 months.

fresh fig, lemon, and strawberry jam

makes 6 half-pints

The second fruit in this quick-and-easy jam can be peaches, nectarines, blueberries, apricots, or whatever is marvelously ripe and sweet at the same time as the figs. My favorite is strawberry.

❧

1½ pounds ripe figs, any variety, stems trimmed, cut into ½-inch pieces

2 pints fresh strawberries, hulled, quartered

2½ cups sugar

¼ cup fresh lemon juice

½ lemon, cut lengthwise, quartered, seeds and white pithy center removed, cut crosswise into thin slices

❧

1. In a large, heavy nonreactive skillet, combine the figs, strawberries, sugar, and lemon juice; mash the fruit with a potato masher. Let stand for at least 1 hour, or up to 2 hours, stirring occasionally.
2. Bring the fruit mixture to a boil over medium-high heat, stirring often. Lower the heat to medium-low and gently boil the jam, stirring often to prevent scorching, until thickened, 20 to 30 minutes. About halfway through the cooking time, use a large metal spoon to skim off any white foam that has accumulated on the surface.
3. Ladle the hot jam through a wide-mouthed funnel into 6 sterilized half-pint jars. Process (see page 154), or simply cover with lids and screw tops and keep refrigerated.

fig and ginger jam

2 pounds ripe figs, any variety, stems trimmed, cut into ½-inch pieces

2½ cups sugar

½ cup coarsely chopped or diced (¼-inch) crystallized ginger

¼ cup fresh lemon juice

½ lemon, cut lengthwise, quartered, seeds and white pithy center removed,
cut crosswise into thin slices

Combine the fruit and flavorings, and proceed as in the preceding recipe.

How to Process Jam

To sterilize the jars, place them in a large pot, cover with water, and heat to boiling. Let stand in the hot water, off the heat, until ready to fill.

While the jam is cooking, place a towel or a wire rack in the bottom of an 8- to 10-quart saucepan. Fill the pan halfway with water and heat to a simmer. Heat a kettle of water to a simmer.

When the jam is ready, lift the jars, using a jar lifter or tongs, from the hot water and drain them on a folded kitchen towel. Using a wide-mouth funnel, fill the jars with the hot jam to within ½ inch of the top. Wipe the jar rims with a clean towel rinsed in hot water. Cover with new rubber-rimmed canning lids and screw the tops on firmly but not too tightly. Using a jar lifter or tongs, place the filled jars in the saucepan of simmering water; do not let the jars touch. Add enough simmering water from the kettle to cover the tops of the jars by about 2 inches. Cover the pan and simmer for 10 minutes. Using the jar lifter or tongs, transfer the jars to a towel to drain. As the jars cool and the seals tighten, you will heat them "ping." Store in a cool, dry place for one year.

fig sources

KALUSTYAN'S
123 Lexington Avenue
New York, NY 10016
212 685 3451
www.kalustyans.com
Premium imported and domestic dried figs.

KNOLL FARMS
Tairwá Produce
Rick and Kristi Knoll
Brentwood, CA 94513
925-634-5959
Kristi@KnollFarms.com
Premium fresh and dried figs; fig wood; fig
    leaves; fig trees.

OREGON EXOTICS NURSERY
1065 Messinger Road
Grants Pass, OR 97527

541-846-7578
www.exoticfruit.com
Many varieties of fig trees for the home
    garden.

RAINTREE NURSERY
391 Butts Road
Morton, WA 98356
www.raintreenursery.com
Many varieties of fig trees for the home
    garden.

VALLEY FIG GROWERS
2028 South Third Street
Fresno, CA 93702
559-237-3893
559-237-3898 (fax)
www.valleyfig.com
Premium fresh and dried figs.

WESTERN FRESH MARKETING
2131 10th Street Suite D
Los Osos, CA 93402
888-820-0001
george@westernfreshmarketing.com
Premium fresh figs

The Internet is a great source of information for the home gardener. I found these two Web sites especially helpful:

www.nafex.org
aggiehorticulture.tamu.edu/extension/ homefruit/fig/fig.html

index

almonds, toasted, chicken, couscous, and dried fig
  salad with, 69–70
amaretto, dried fig sauce with, 147
apple:
  baked, stuffed with dried figs and walnuts,
    140–41
  and dried fig-stuffed pork loin with cider sauce,
    85–86
  oatmeal and dried fig crisp, 107–8
  salad with dried figs, Parmigiano-Reggiano, and
    walnuts, 56–57
apricots.
  and dried figs in vanilla wine syrup, 139
  in fresh figs and summer fruits in honey wine
    syrup with lemon thyme,
    131–32
artichokes, lamb stew with dried figs and, 81–82
arugula, grilled fresh fig salad with cantaloupe,
  fennel, and walnuts, 52–53

Asiago cheese and fresh fig frittata,
  32–33

bacon:
  fresh fig and frisée salad with goat cheese and,
    54–55
  -wrapped wine-poached dried figs, 23–24
balsamic vinegar:
  in the classic fig drizzle, 58
  sautéed fresh figs with, 8
banana:
  in dried fig smoothie, 100
  walnut and dried fig muffins, 115–16
basil, fresh fig and green tomato salad with, 51
biscotti, dried fig and chocolate, 117–18
blueberry(ies):
  in flourless dried fig and chocolate cake with fig
    custard sauce, 110–11

blueberry(ies) (*continued*)

in fresh figs and summer fruits in honey wine
    syrup with lemon thyme, 131–32

and fresh fig tart, 102

blue cheese, in dried fig and black olive spread for
    crostini, 19–20

bonbons, dried fig, orange, and chocolate,
    137–38

bulgur with walnuts and dried figs, 90–91

cake, dried fig and chocolate, flourless, with fig
    custard sauce, 110–11

candied orange–flavored figs, 7

cantaloupe:

in fresh figs and summer fruits in honey wine
    syrup with lemon thyme, 131–32

grilled fresh fig salad with fennel, arugula,
    walnuts and, 52–53

caramel:

and fresh fig sauce for ice cream, 146

orange sauce, fresh figs with mascarpone and,
    129

Cheddar cheese, in bacon-wrapped wine-poached
    dried figs, 23–24

cheese:

and dried fig cocktail crescents, 25–26

and figs, combination of, 26

and figs sandwich, open-faced, 41

-filled fresh figs, 27–28

open-faced dried fig and melted, sandwiches,
    40–41

-stuffed figs, 7

see also specific cheeses

chicken:

braised, with fennel and dried figs, 63–64

breasts stuffed with fresh figs and goat cheese,
    65–66

couscous, and dried fig salad with toasted
    almonds, 69–70

thighs, curried, with dried figs and tomatoes,
    67–68

chocolate:

chunky, dried fig, and pecan cookies, 121–22

dried fig, and orange bonbons, 137–38

and dried fig biscotti, 117–18

and dried fig cake, flourless, with fig custard
    sauce, 110

-stuffed fresh figs with vanilla custard sauce,
    135–36

chocolate, bittersweet:

in dried fig, orange, and chocolate bonbons,
    137–38

in dried fig and chocolate biscotti, 117–18

chocolate, semisweet:

in chocolate-stuffed fresh figs with vanilla custard
    sauce, 135–36

in chunky chocolate, dried fig, and pecan
    cookies, 121–22

in dried fig, walnut, and chunky chip sugar
    cookies, 123–24

in flourless dried fig and chocolate cake with fig
    custard sauce, 110–11

chunky chip, dried fig, and walnut sugar cookies,
    123–24

cider sauce, dried fig and apple-stuffed pork loin
    with, 85–86

cinnamon:

dried fig scones, 113–14

ice cream with dried fig ripple,
    142–43

clafouti, fresh fig, 109

classic fig drizzle, 58

Comté cheese:

    in open-faced dried fig and melted cheese sandwiches, 40–41

    warm fresh fig salad with Black Forest ham and, 49–50

cookies:

    chunky chocolate, dried fig, and pecan, 121–22

    dried fig, walnut, and chunky chip sugar, 123–24

    homemade fig newtons, 125–26

    Nana's fig stuffed, 119–20

couscous, chicken, and dried fig salad with toasted almonds, 69–70

cream cheese, dried fig, and walnut spread, 21–22

    with smoked salmon, 22

crescents, cocktail, dried fig and cheese, 25–26

crostini:

    dried fig and black olive spread for, 19–20

    fig, 8

    with quick fig jam and warm herbed goat cheese, 17–18

crumble, fresh fig and peach, 105–6

custard sauce:

    fig, 112

    vanilla, chocolate-stuffed fresh figs with, 135–36

dessert, simple fig, 8

dough, pizza, 46

dried fig(s), 6–7

    and apple oatmeal crisp, 107–8

    apple salad with Parmigiano-Reggiano, walnuts and, 56–57

    and apple-stuffed pork loin with cider sauce, 85–86

    and apricots in vanilla wine syrup, 139

    bacon-wrapped wine-poached, 23–24

    baked apples stuffed with walnuts and, 140–41

    and banana walnut muffins, 115–16

    and black olive spread for crostini, 19–20

    braised chicken with fennel and, 63–64

    bulgur with walnuts and, 90–91

    and cheese cocktail crescents, 25–26

    in cheese-filled fresh figs variation, 28

    chicken, and couscous salad with toasted almonds, 69–70

    and chocolate biscotti, 117–18

    and chocolate cake, flourless, with fig custard sauce, 110–11

    chopping of, 138

    chunky chocolate and pecan cookies, 121–22

    cinnamon scones, 113–14

    cream cheese, and walnut spread, 21–22

    cream cheese, and walnut spread with smoked salmon, 22

    curried chicken thighs with tomatoes and, 67–68

    or fresh, walnut and rosemary focaccia, 42–43

    in homemade fig newtons, 125–26

    lamb stew with artichokes and, 81–82

    and melted cheese sandwiches, open-faced, 40–41

    in Nana's fig-stuffed cookies, 119–20

    orange, and chocolate bonbons, 137–38

    orange, fennel, and sweet onion salad with mixed greens, 47–48

    oven-roasted halibut with onions, orange and fresh or, 77–78

    poached, in phyllo flowers with spiced syrup, 127–28

    quick ideas for, 7

    and red pepper sauce over ricotta salata, 34–35

dried fig(s) (*continued*)

ripple, cinnamon ice cream with, 142–43

roasted root vegetables with wine-plumped, 94–95

sauce with amaretto, 147

smoothie, 100

walnut, and chunky chip sugar cookies, 123–24

duck legs, pan-braised, with Marsala and fresh fig jam, 73–74

endive leaves with fresh fig salsa and goat cheese, 36

fennel:

braised chicken with dried figs and, 63–64

dried fig, orange, and sweet onion salad with mixed greens, 47–48

fresh fig–stuffed pork loin with onions and, 83–84

grilled fresh fig salad with cantaloupe, arugula, and walnuts, 52–53

feta cheese:

in dried fig and black olive spread for crostini, 19–20

in grilled or oven-baked fresh fig, olive, and caramelized onion flatbreads, 44–45

fettuccine with lemon, rosemary, and fresh figs, 87–88

fig(s):

in Bible and history, 2

botany and cultivation of, 3–6

love and, 3

varieties and seasons of, 10, 11

see also dried fig(s), fresh fig(s)

fig jam:

fresh, lemon, and strawberry, 153

fresh, pan-braised duck legs with Marsala and, 73–74

ginger and, 154

quick, crostini with warm herbed goat cheese and, 17–18

fig leaves, 2, 12–14

salmon and potatoes roasted on, with fresh fig salad, 75–76

flatbreads, grilled or oven-baked fresh fig, olive, and caramelized onion, 44–45

focaccia, fresh or dried fig, walnut and rosemary, 42–43

Fontina cheese, in open-faced dried fig and melted cheese sandwiches, 40–41

fresh fig(s), 9–10

and Asiago cheese frittata, 32–33

and blueberry tart, 102

and caramel sauce for ice cream, 146

cheese-filled, 27–28

chicken breasts stuffed with goat cheese and, 65–66

chocolate-stuffed, with vanilla custard sauce, 135–36

clafouti, 109

classic drizzle, 58

or dried, walnut, and rosemary focaccia, 42–43

fast ideas for, 8

fettuccine with lemon, and rosemary, 87–88

freezing of, 152

and frisée salad with goat cheese and bacon, 54–55

fritters, warm, 133

greens, mixed (*continued*)

    dried fig, orange, fennel, and sweet onion salad
        with, 47–48

Gruyère cheese:

    in open-faced dried fig and melted cheese
        sandwiches, 40–41

    in warm fresh fig salad with Comté cheese and
        Black Forest ham, 49–50

halibut, oven-roasted, with onions, orange, and
    fresh or dried figs, 77–78

ham:

    Black Forest, warm fresh fig salad with Comté
        cheese and, 49–50

    in grilled pig n' fig sandwich, 41

honey:

    -glazed game hens with lemon and fresh figs,
        71–72

    in grilled fresh figs on rosemary skewers, 29–30

    vanilla syrup, 134

    -vanilla wine syrup, fresh fruit in, 132

    wine syrup with lemon thyme, fresh figs and
        summer fruits in, 131–32

ice cream:

    cinnamon, with dried fig ripple,
        142–43

    fresh fig and caramel sauce for, 146

    makers, 143

lamb stew with artichokes and dried figs, 81–82

leeks, in braised chicken with fennel and dried figs,
    63–64

lemon:

    fettuccine with rosemary, fresh figs and,
        87–88

    fresh fig, and strawberry jam, 153

    honey-glazed game hens with fresh figs and,
        71–72

lemon thyme:

    fresh figs and summer fruits in honey wine syrup
        with, 131–32

    in salmon and potatoes roasted on fig leaves with
        fresh fig salad, 75–76

lime and fresh fig sorbet, 144

marinated figs, 7

Marsala, pan-braised duck legs with fresh fig jam
    and, 73–74

mascarpone, fresh figs with orange caramel sauce
    and, 129

mozzarella, in grilled or oven-baked fresh fig, olive,
    and caramelized onion flatbreads, 44–45

muffins, dried fig and banana walnut, 115–16

Nana's fig-stuffed cookies, 119–20

nectarines:

    in fresh figs and summer fruits in honey wine
        syrup with lemon thyme,
        131–32

    in fresh fig smoothie, 99

oatmeal apple and dried fig crisp, 107–8

olive:

    black, and dried fig spread for crostini,
        19–20